THE LONDON HISTORY STUDIES   NUMBER 2

General Editor: R.Ben Jones B.LITT. M.A.

Advisory Panel

W.G.Barr M.A. Fellow and Senior Tutor, Exeter College, Oxford;
Lecturer in Modern History, University of Oxford

Alun Davies M.A. Professor of Modern History, University College of
Swansea

J.R.Hale M.A. Professor of History, University of Warwick

C.P.Hill M.A. Senior Lecturer in Education, University of Exeter

Marjorie Reeves M.A. PH.D. Fellow and Tutor in Modern History,
St Anne's College, Oxford; Lecturer in Modern History,
University of Oxford

G.A.Williams M.A. PH.D. Professor of History, University of York

The American War of
Independence

PETER WELLS M.A.

UNIVERSITY OF LONDON PRESS LTD

SBN 340 06049 2 Boards
SBN 340 06054 9 Paper

Copyright © 1967 Peter Wells
Maps copyright © 1967 University of London Press Ltd

University of London Press Ltd
St Paul's House, Warwick Lane, London EC4

Designed by Gerald Wilkinson
Printed and bound in Great Britain by
Hazell Watson & Viney Ltd, Aylesbury, Bucks

EDITOR'S INTRODUCTION

THE LONDON HISTORY STUDIES are designed expressly for sixth-form students. They examine those events and personalities of the last five hundred years which continue to attract the attention of historians and arouse argument among them.

The books in the series are intended to be succinct and concentrated. Short quotations from contemporary sources are used both to enliven the text and to produce evidence to support particular arguments, while the differing views of the principal historians are fairly represented. In addition to the facts, students should find a clear statement of the problems involved in each subject, presented in such a way as to ensure understanding and to stimulate thought. Short bibliographies give direction to further research.

The authors are practising sixth-form teachers who have been asked to write on the subjects in which they are especially interested. They are naturally familiar with the current research in their chosen fields, but they can in addition draw on the knowledge and experience of the scholars and leading historians who compose the Advisory Panel. Thus the books contain the fruits of modern scholarship and are written from a close acquaintance with the questions that occur to students and the difficulties that face them.

It is hoped that this series will provide not only vigorous and effective treatment of the topics under discussion, but also an aid to a clear understanding of the methods of the historian.

R.B.J.

CONTENTS

MAPS

PART I
The Colonial Background

INTRODUCTION: BRITISH OPINION AND AMERICA

Before 1765 Englishmen were generally indifferent to American affairs. Ignorance lay at the root of this attitude. Tales of early exploration were still popular and people were aware of the continent across the Atlantic, but only vaguely and then only because of its association with other activities such as French wars or trade. Sailors and merchants visited the colonies, but few travelled inland. Trading was possible without undue intimacy, and in some cases the Americans were equally indifferent to their British counterparts. Yet gossip, politics and business news were brought back and recounted in the coffee houses or taverns of the great ports, Bristol, Liverpool and London in particular.

Commerce was the true bond between America and Britain before 1763. Parliament regulated trade through the Navigation Acts, a system which was generally acceptable to all concerned. Trade stimulated manufacturing and involved, among others, the ribbon weavers of Coventry and the potters of Staffordshire, as well as the more stately silversmiths and watchmakers, in production for the American market. During the eighteenth century the volume of trade expanded and British capital invested in the colonies increased. Some business enterprises failed, and Englishmen were occasionally disenchanted with the colonial dream, while others feared colonial competition. In general, however, men felt favourably disposed towards the colonies if trade continued to flow.

The country gentry were not so concerned with the American colonies provided these did not affect their pockets. Heavy taxation, through the class obligation of the Land Tax, was a primary grievance but they were also obliged to pay local poor rates which became heavy in times of bad harvests or unemployment. Landed gentry, strongly represented in Parliament, feared in 1763 that America, which now included Canada, would become an additional financial burden. They looked closely at the system of colonial enterprise and saw profits going to the merchants while they would be expected to bear the cost of administering this vast domain. The gentry exerted pressure on the ministry to obtain redress.

Therefore a new policy of taxation was introduced whereby the colonies were expected to contribute towards their upkeep. This brought the British and the Americans into conflict for the first time. By 1765 it was necessary for a well-informed Englishman to have opinions about America. Controversy stirred the embers of enquiry. Ex-governors of colonies, like Thomas Pownall of Massachusetts, wrote weighty tomes; maps of North America and copies of the original colonial charters were printed and eagerly bought at the bookshops; pamphlets, a staple diet of the literary and political scene, appeared to argue one case or another. The growth of newspapers in the period (1760 – circulation about 9,500,000 annually; 1782 – about 15,250,000) is partly attributable to public interest in American affairs. The *Middlesex Journal* attacked the government mercilessly; the *Royal Gazette* loyally supported successive ministries. Other events, especially the John Wilkes affair, stimulated political debate and in the 1760s the liberty of the press was a reality.

Attitudes towards the American colonies crystallized. Some resentment was felt that British emigrants were stock that could ill be spared by the mother country. Colonial prosperity was represented as Utopian. With the removal of the French security was assured, apart from occasional Indian disturbances. General support for making Americans pay additional taxes emerged. Propaganda soon obscured facts on both sides of the Atlantic. Also attitudes varied according to personal interests. If you were a merchant you would be against additional taxation because this impeded the flow of trade. If you were a lawyer you would ponder the issues of parliamentary representation and the nature of sovereignty. If you were a squire in Somerset you would gladly be rid of some costs which Americans could well afford. Increasingly common to all shades of opinion was the feeling that Parliament could not be defied indefinitely by her colonies. By 1773 order appeared to be dissolving into anarchy. Patriotism was then a glorious rallying cry and when war came in 1775 it was estimated that four out of five Englishmen were against the Americans.

For their part, Americans did not think of themselves as Americans but rather as Englishmen or Germans, Virginians or New Yorkers, depending on their nationality and colony. An awareness of trans-Atlantic nationalism barely existed in 1763 and only slowly evolved as opposition to Britain seemed more necessary. Even so the majority remained unmoved by the controversy and deplored the factious nature of the age. Colonial separation remained intense and commentators have remarked on the thirteen wars of independence waged in 1775. Yet cooperation, organization and determination were characteristics which developed fitfully between 1763 and 1775. The colonies were coming of age.

[1] THE GEOGRAPHICAL LOCATION

By 1775 there were thirty-one British colonies in the Americas. Eighteen of these were on the mainland from Quebec in the north to East Florida in the south; thirteen were in the islands of the West Indies. The best known are the thirteen continental colonies which rebelled and achieved independence in 1783, but it is important to realize that they were not the sole British possessions, nor did some commentators believe them to be the most profitable or worthy of salvage. The hindsight of a later century should not mislead us to expect to find New York as a thriving metropolis challenging London in 1775 – it had only 20,000 inhabitants compared to London's some 800,000 – nor to expect ministers of the Crown to speed communiqués to Washington, a city which did not so far exist.

The greatest wealth lay in the West Indies and, especially after the defeat at Saratoga in 1777, the British war machine was geared to prevent the loss of the islands and Canada as much as crush the rebels. The colonies along the eastern seabord – New Hampshire, Massachusetts, Connecticut, Rhode Island, New York, New Jersey, Pennsylvania, Delaware, Maryland, Virginia, North and South Carolina and Georgia – had often proved difficult to control either politically or economically; their strong-headed independence owed much to the fact that the majority of the inhabitants were of English stock, though the minority groups of Scotch/Irish from Ulster, Dutch, Germans and Swedes had an equally determined stake in the future. By 1763 Great Britain could claim that the lands east of the Mississippi were indisputably her own, the result of one hundred and fifty years of intermittent endeavour by the Crown against European rivals. To all intents and purposes a golden age of prosperity and goodwill among English-speaking peoples was about to occur; the prosperity was certainly achieved eventually, but at the expense of goodwill.

In these eastern regions the Appalachian mountains are the most dominant geographical feature on the mainland. They are some 300 miles broad and 1,500 miles long, densely wooded, affording only one major gap in the whole range. This was a considerable barrier to expansion, but it also gave security; for example, the Indian nations of the east were separated from their fellows in the Mississippi valley who could have proved far more of a problem for the early settlers. Also the mountains were protection from the French. They compelled the English to concentrate their efforts on the easily worked coastal strip or the eastern foothills of the mountains rather than plunge into the vast unknown beyond. This geographical limitation helped political and economic development.

The coastal strip is only 50 to 80 miles wide in New England

but in the Carolinas it becomes 250 miles broad; fertility was far
greater in the south and the character of the colonies was much
influenced by the quality of the soil. Farming was tougher in the
north so there was a great incentive to earn a livelihood from the
forests, especially in New Hampshire, or to fish and trade. Southern soils were easier to work, the climate altogether more favourable. Landholdings sprawled in Virginia and since land was cheap
no care was taken to conserve the soil. So the foothills of the
mountains were cleared and by 1750 it was the Virginians who
were most anxious to cross the Appalachians and plunge into the
Ohio valley. In pursuing this policy they incurred the military
opposition of the French.

The largest gap in the range is the Hudson River – Lake
Champlain route to the St Lawrence or the Hudson – Mohawk
river route to the Great Lakes. In time of war the control of the
Hudson, with New York at its eastern exit to the sea becomes
crucial. The French in Canada feared it as a possible route for
British aggression; the Americans in the War of Independence
saw that British control of the river would effectively cut communications between New England and the south. Rivers generally are significant in the geography of North America. The in-
dented coastline offered landing facilities to the first settlers and
natural harbours for their trading vessels; they also encouraged
exploration inland in a search for farms and furs. Probably the
St Lawrence is the best example, but the enormous area of
Chesapeake Bay with the James, Potomac and Susquehanna
rivers flowing into it is of equal importance. The wealth of rivers
and harborage gave an impetus to ship building and commerce,
the development of which brought a considerable financial return.

Within the British possessions there was immense diversity of
geographical conditions: in Quebec the shorter summers and
bitterly cold winters contrasted with the heat and humidity of
the West Indies with their hurricanes and tropical diseases, factors which undermined military calculations in the war. Within
the thirteen colonies themselves the differences were marked.
The area of Maine, an integral part of Massachusetts, was tem-
perate with rock-strewn coastline; Georgia was subtropical with

extensive swamplands to the south. In the same way crops reflect these differences: tobacco, indigo dye, and rice were as distinctly southern as later cotton was to become. The ease of farming in the south led to a search for labour and the Negro slave seemed ideal. The white man was considered ill-suited to manual labour for long periods under a hot sun; the Negro could not only work well in such conditions, but was believed to resist the diseases of the ricefields more easily. The plantation system could not have operated without him.

Thus geography was an important factor in the development of the colonies, how men worked and where they moved. The European immigrant found the climate of the middle colonies most congenial, but everywhere there was an opportunity to prosper. A geographical unity was apparent and was partly responsible for the quick response of the colonists to government legislation after 1763, initially when a halt was called to expansion westwards over the Appalachians.

[2] THE NORTHERN COLONIES

The northernmost colonies of Quebec, Nova Scotia and Newfoundland did not rebel. The most important of these was Quebec, captured from the French in 1759, maintained under military rule until 1763 and then given civil government as a province. Surprise was expressed at the peace terms when the British kept Canada rather than the sugar island of Guadeloupe in the West Indies. The situation was that the planters feared excess sugar production and the French were prepared to withdraw from North America, so Canada did not become a bargaining point. The population was composed of 70,000 French-speaking and Roman Catholic whites and about 7,600 Indians. The ambition of the British was to encourage English-speaking settlers and gradually remodel the area as an English colony. Retired soldiers, for example, received free grants of land, and attractive conditions were offered to entice families from the south. The area attracted few settlers and those who did arrive preferred trade or innkeeping to farming; by 1764 there were only 200 'Protestant housekeepers' in the cities of Quebec and Montreal. Numbers grew slowly but fell off after 1770, only to grow when loyalists fled from the rebels so that by 1788 there were 21,000 English-speaking people in a population of 130,000.

Between 1763 and 1774 the future of the province was un-settled. No legislative council was established because there were so few Protestants or Englishmen, the only men eligible to vote since the Test Acts, debarring Roman Catholics from public life, operated in the colonies. This exclusion weakened the judicial bench and all other aspects of provincial administration. The governor and his council carefully conciliated French opinion and every effort was made to respect French customs, both legal and religious, while the future of the colony was discussed in London. The lack of urgency was appalling but in 1766 a Canadian bishop consecrated in France was accepted by the British government. The failure to create a popular assembly was bitterly criticized by the English merchants who claimed they lived under a military and French tyranny. The colony unhappily divided into factions and the governor, Murray, was recalled in 1766 for failing to please in an impossible situation; his successor, Guy Carleton, Lord Dorchester, remained in Canada for thirty years. The Quebec Act of 1774 was an astute document, but even that seemed in some instances to be a provisional measure.

Acadia had been ceded to the British in 1713 at the peace of Utrecht and renamed Nova Scotia. The French population declined and by 1766 represented only 500 in a total of 11,200. Inducements were offered to New Englanders to settle; they arrived swiftly so that by 1775 there were 20,000 inhabitants, but the colony, burdened with debt, was maintained by the Crown through the troubles, receiving direct financial aid from Parliament.

All French claims to Newfoundland had been relinquished in 1713, but English law was spasmodic and hardly enforceable. By 1765 the vast majority of the 20,000 inhabitants were concerned in the cod fishing industry and it was the task of the governor, a naval officer, to protect the legitimate rights of the islanders against both the French and the New Englanders. The island was quite prosperous and consumed over a half of Massachusetts's rum production in return for fish, furs and imported European goods.

Of the most northerly colonies which resisted the Crown in 1775, three had strong Puritan religious backgrounds and the fourth was a haven from religious persecution. The most influential of these New England colonies was Massachusetts. By 1775 it had the largest white population of all American colonies, 355,000, although Virginia with its Negroes totalled 500,000; its major city, Boston, was third largest with 15,500 people; and by 1765 it had 200 townships, all potential centres of agitation. But the colony was more than just numerically superior. It was the centre of American mercantile enterprise, of Protestant Bible-conscious religion, of articulate men who valued their freedom highly in all spheres of activity; the determination of such men unified the colony in its protest against alleged tyranny.

Boston had been the focal point of New World trade, though by 1775 its position was usurped by Philadelphia and further threatened by the expansion of New York. In New England Boston flourished supreme as the centre of the shipbuilding industry, the molasses and rum traffic (there were 60 distilleries producing over $2\frac{1}{2}$ million gallons per annum), the fisheries, marketing of slaves, and coastal traffic. In order to further these interests the New Englanders travelled all over the globe but especially in the North Atlantic where the trading between England, Africa, the West Indies and Boston or Newport, Rhode Island, brought a favourable financial reward. The merchants of Boston were directly threatened by British legislation after 1763 as this was designed to eliminate smuggling, a major factor in colonial wealth, and rigorously to control the operation of trade through an improved customs service.

Life in Massachusetts was governed, in theory at least, by the Calvinist church, though an increasingly secular trend in society was noticeable throughout the eighteenth century. The dominance of religious belief stemmed from the Pilgrim Fathers whose ship the *Mayflower* reached Cape Cod in November 1620. The community was comprised of English Puritans who had separated from the Anglican church and, failing to begin new lives satisfactorily in Holland, had decided for social and economic reasons, to emigrate to the New World. Originally they planned to settle within the colony of Virginia, but driven off course they stayed in the more northerly lands and founded the colony of New Plymouth, later absorbed by Massachusetts.

Yet Massachusetts itself was founded in 1630 by Puritans who sought to establish an ideal community of godly people far from the influence of the British crown. The activities of Archbishop Laud and the Arminians in England prior to 1640 led to extensive emigration. They created a community with church and state closely integrated, where toleration or democracy were forbidden and a strict moral code prevailed. The strength of these congregationalist churches was immense and the missionary zeal of the members considerable; new towns formed around the churches and the population steadily increased. The self-government of the churches certainly helped to develop independence of mind, despite the fear of political democracy, but the often narrow social outlook of the congregations conflicted increasingly with the commercial spirit. Puritanism remained an important feature in the lives of the settlers, more so in smaller communities than in large towns, and it was commonly believed that the success of the people bore witness to the pleasure of the Almighty.

Connecticut was likewise founded by Puritans, in 1662. By contrast with Massachusetts it was predominantly rural but, considering its size, by 1775 supported a large population of 199,000. As in Massachusetts, the Congregational church was established by law and the same moral ideals operated. Yet the colony was completely self-governing, a feature shared with neighbouring Rhode Island and which distinguished them both from all other colonies in America. Generally the political and social lead in New England was taken by Massachusetts with the result that New Hampshire, a royal colony since 1679 and a large wood-producing area, together with Connecticut followed suit.

Rhode Island was initially different because religious toleration for all Protestants was the cornerstone of its constitution. A Congregationalist minister, Roger Williams, had been banished from Massachusetts in 1636 and founded the town of Providence. Settlers who felt that toleration was a condition of the ideal society, joined him; so successful was the venture that the area achieved recognition as a separate and self-governing colony at the Restoration of Charles II. By 1775 the 60,000 strong colony had gained an unenviable reputation in official circles for its smuggling activities, for the manner by which government was carried on in comparative secrecy, and for the aid given to the French during the Seven Years' War. The mercantile wealth was undoubted and excited jealousy among some Bostonian competitors, especially as the absence of a royal customs service made smuggling so easy.

The most prominent features of these colonies were their concern for religious affairs, their Englishness, their mercantile interest and the development of town councils where political debate could flourish. Tocqueville wrote later:

The civilization of New England has been like a beacon lit upon a hill, which, after it has diffused its warmth around, tinges the distant horizon with its glow.

The manner in which the New England people maintained their religion and material interests deserves this tribute, although Tocqueville perhaps overestimates the social warmth of their Puritanical faith.

The demarcation which traditionally divides the northern from the southern colonies is the Mason–Dixon line. Running along latitude 39° 43′ N it determines the southern boundary of Pennsylvania and the northern of Maryland. Later it became the distinction between slave and free states, but in the eighteenth century slavery was universal in the Americas and the line was more useful to determine the northerly extent of plantation farming. Although a Quaker had founded Pennsylvania, religious fervour was not an obvious characteristic of colonial life outside New England. The Penn family kept its proprietary interests, despite their change to the Anglican faith and the wrath of Quaker merchants who formed a mercantile aristocracy. By 1775 there were 300,000 inhabitants and the colony could boast the largest city on the continent, Philadelphia, with 40,000 inhabitants – no wonder Howe wished to secure the city in 1776. Various advantages attracted settlers: first, the soil was rich and was sold at bargain prices; secondly, there was a great diversity of economic enterprise – farming, industry and trade – and the financial affairs of the colony were sound; thirdly, the government was benevolent, religious toleration was extended to all, and taxation was minimal. For the Germans in particular the colony seemed to offer paradise. Men from the Rhineland, tired of ceaseless war, came to live in peace; so many of them arrived that the German language was second only to English.

Yet conflict existed in paradise. The Quaker merchants in the east refused to listen to the demands of the western frontiersmen for protection; they considered the Indian problem was best settled peacefully and declined to vote money for defence. Pontiac's rising of 1763 threatened to destroy the frontiersmen so in 1764 they marched to Philadelphia. The men called themselves the Paxton Boys and gained support from the popular leaders in the city but the Quakers were able to persuade the marchers to return home. Nothing was done to meet their petitions. This clash of interests was frequently repeated in other colonies, especially involving the coast settlers and backwoodsmen. Such lack of unity as was evident from the Paxton Boys' rising and the Regulator movement in the Carolinas made the British task during the war less hopeless than might otherwise have been the case. Certainly the Pennsylvanians displayed greater enthusiasm for arguing among themselves than fighting the British. This contrasts vividly with the cohesion in Massachusetts.

Potentially the most loyal to the Crown of the northern colonies was New York, ruled by an oligarchy conscious of its aristocratic nature and privileges, faced with an Indian problem because the Six Nations held land within its boundaries. This meant that British regular troops were essential in maintaining a defensive system. The large landowners were exceedingly rich. They traced their ancestry back to the original Dutch settlers or to the favourites of the Duke of York who captured New Amsterdam in 1664. The colony had been renamed in honour of the conqueror. Such familes closely watched their affairs and their power increased rather than diminished in the eighteenth century especially because they were prepared to marry into the wealthy and influential professional or merchant families of New York city. Land for the new settlers was hard to come by and the population, despite the large acreage, was only 182,000 by 1775. Not only land but power was denied to the less sophisticated – the qualifications to vote were prohibitive; £40 freehold was the requirement (£2 in Connecticut); the House of Representatives consisted of 31 members (152 in Connecticut) and nearly all were connected with the landowners. The feudal structure of the colony lent support to the British cause and nearly half the state was tory during the War of Independence. New York city was most important – it offered an excellent harbour and was linked with Canada via the Hudson River, the only route open for twelve months of the year. Its capture in 1776 made it the centre of British activity.

The remaining two colonies played a less positive role in the war. New Jersey had become a royal colony in 1702 but suffered from considerable internal rioting between 1755 and 1765. Land claims were in utter confusion and a tense struggle between large and small landholders developed. After 1765 order and prosperity returned. The men of New Jersey were drawn into the revolutionary struggle through the pressure of their neighbours rather than any positive dissatisfaction with the colonial system. Delaware, earlier a Swedish settlement, possessed a separate legislature but shared a governor with Pennsylvania and was very much under the influence of that colony.

THE AMERICAN POSSESSIONS, 1763–83
(*adapted from Muir's Historical Atlas*)

[3] THE SOUTHERN COLONIES

The distinction between northern and southern colonies may be
summed up in the concept of the plantation. Based on an estate
devoted to staple crops, employing Negro slaves and enjoying a
more sunny climate, the way of life on a southern plantation was
more relaxed. In the north, a constant battle with the elements
produced a more varied economy, with the greatest wealth found
in the towns. Leaders in the south were landowners; northern
worthies were merchants or traders. The Anglican church flourished in the south, whereas nonconformity was usual elsewhere.
Southerners distrusted the democratic tendencies in New England, where it was commonly believed that Virginians were the
very stuff of impiety with their dancing, drinking and gay clothes.
Yet jealousies and distinctions existed as much between individual colonies as between the two sections. Georgians were not
highly regarded in Virginia, nor Rhode Islanders in Massachusetts.
This divisive tendency was certainly recognized by the British
government but might have been even more skilfully exploited.

Virginia was the queen of the South, if not of all the British
possessions on the mainland. Here the earliest attempts at colonization had been made in the reign of the Virgin Queen, Elizabeth.
In 1606 the Virginia Company was formed and the first settlement achieved under Captain John White at Jamestown, in
1607; tobacco soon became the dominant concern and source of
wealth. Negro slaves were introduced to fulfil the need for labour.
Large-scale plantations grew at the expense of smaller mixed
economy farms. Great capital was required; the slave system led
to friction between the larger and lesser farmers throughout the
South; vested interests usually prevailed. The Virginians were
sturdily independent of England but ties did exist – all tobacco
had to be traded overseas through English ports, the Church of
England was established by law and planter debts accumulated
in London. Despite considerable apparent wealth, the expenditure of the rich in a socially conscious community exceeded their
income. Jefferson reckoned in 1775 that some £2 million were due

to British merchants. Crops were mortgaged ahead but the low price of tobacco ensured that debts were never reduced. These planters were an aristocracy, not by European standards perhaps, but together with their peers in Charleston they gave the South its culture, pride and leadership frequently envied by those who could not compete.

The backcountry of Virginia, in Piedmont and the Shenandoah valley, contained 200,000 of the 300,000 whites in the colony. Here Negro slavery was on a lesser scale and the forces of democracy more apparent. Whereas the coastal aristocracy was of English origin, the valley was predominantly German or Scotch/ Irish. The House of Burgesses in the 1760s reflected the querulous nature of the colonists, influenced by demagogues like Patrick Henry or the discontented younger aristocrat, Richard Henry Lee.

Maryland's economy was similarly based on the plantation system but not on such a grandiose scale. The colony was proprietary, belonging to Lord Baltimore, but the local Assembly was as constantly in conflict with the family as were the Pennsylvanians with the Penns. It had no need of defence forces, nor did it have any Indian problems, so was most reluctant to contribute towards the cost of such ventures; indeed during the Seven Years' War it was obstructive and begrudging in the extreme.

North and South Carolina boasted their planter aristocracy and slave labour force along the coastal belt, though especially in the south. Charleston was the fourth largest city in the thirteen colonies and undoubtedly the finest in the south.

In grandeur, splendour of buildings, decorations, equipages, numbers, shippings and indeed in almost everything, it far surpasses all I ever saw, or expected to see, in America.

So wrote Josiah Quincey Jr. This capital offered a rich and cultured life, with a pleasing climate, to government officials and the exclusive set of merchants and planters who were often contemptuous of their North Carolinian neighbours. The planter princes all lived in the tideway area, growing rice or indigo, ignoring the affairs of the interior in both colonies; corruption, lack of justice, high taxation and absence of representation in the assemblies were bitterly resented. Regulator associations formed in 1768 to force a remedy and violence flared up in North Carolina in 1770. In 1771 the Regulators were defeated by the militia at the battle of Alamance; the ringleaders were hanged but many fled westwards to avoid punishment or subjection. In South Carolina the protagonists did not resort to violence because concessions were made by the administration. Yet the differences between the planter and the backwoodsman, engaged on his harvest of pitch, turpentine and other naval stores, remained unresolved. Nonetheless the colourful social life of Charleston flourished until the Civil War of 1861.

Whereas the Carolinas had a joint population of 470,000, the colony of Georgia could boast but 33,000 of whom 15,000 were slaves. Founded in 1732 as a haven for English gentlemen debtors it became a royal colony in 1754. The ground was suitable for plantation crops yet a Parliamentary grant of £3,000 per annum aided an economy which, given a reasonable exertion on the part of the Assembly, could have been self-sufficient.

To the south of Georgia the British controlled East and West Florida and the islands of the West Indies. The population of the Floridas was very small, only 120 whites in the East, and 5,000 in the West centred on the townships of Mobile and Pensacola. A representative assembly met in the West but neither area could be called self-sufficient. The territory, gained from Spain in 1763, was returned to her in 1783 and then bought by the United States in 1819.

The West Indies were the southern colonies Englishmen most prized and over which they held most control. The main crop was sugar and in the eighteenth century it was Jamaica which rose to predominate in its production and to support the largest population, 236,000 by 1787. Yet the fortunes of the islands were by no means assured because competition from both Spanish and French colonies threatened to undercut prices. The government protected sugar production by the Molasses Act of 1733, whereby prohibitive duties throughout the Empire were levied on imported foreign rum, sugar or molasses, and the Sugar Act of 1739, which allowed the free export of British sugar directly to foreign ports. This latter helped to keep prices favourably high for the planters, but the former remained a dead letter since the difficulties of enforcement were so enormous. Seven to ten per cent was considered a good financial return on one's capital and this was maintained through the heyday of the plantations, 1749–56. European war had cut back French competition, but the main reason for prosperity was the growing demand for sugar in England which created higher prices. Although the French product was often 50 per cent cheaper than the English, mercantilist principles forbad its importation. Production continued to expand, exports to Britain rising from 130 million pounds in 1763 to 190 million in 1774. Obviously this was a vast machine with future potential.

Considerable ties existed between the islands and the mainland colonies. American merchants could conveniently supply foodstuffs and raw materials most cheaply; they were also slavers, and on the journey north took molasses to supply the rum distilleries of New England. Yet there was always the temptation for Americans to buy their sugar illegally from French sources at lower cost. This was most frequently the case, so that evasion of the mercantile acts was more noteworthy than compliance with their provisions. The entire molasses output of the West Indies did not equal two-thirds of the quantity imported into Rhode Island. Americans felt no compunction in evading a law so obviously designed by the West Indian lobby in Parliament to advance their own interests against those of the mainland colonists. But many planters were in debt, often to Americans, but also to Englishmen. Nonetheless the ostentation of planters who returned home was proverbial. Links which bound the islanders, the colonists and the English merchants together were strong, in so far as there was a mutual desire to avoid war as much as the late summer hurricanes.

[4] COLONIAL GOVERNMENT

Eight of the thirteen colonies were the direct responsibility of the Crown. This meant that a governor, council and officials were appointed in London. These men were under oath to the king and regarded him as the source of their authority and were his agents in the New World. Yet all the colonies were ultimately subject to the Crown, even the corporation colonies of Rhode Island and Connecticut, who elected their own governor, and the proprietary colonies of Pennsylvania, Delaware and Maryland, where the family chose the governor. In the situation whereby geographical distances, local ideology and racial composition all tended to isolate communities, after 1688 this common denominator of allegiance to the Crown, together with acceptance of the basic ideas of English law and procedure, provided a degree of political unity. Though not always acceptable, the link with the Crown was stronger than that between individual colonies. Apart from the Albany plan of 1754 no move was made by the colonists to unite until the period of imperial reorganization after 1763. Powers of the Crown and its officials were limited by the presence in all these colonies of popularly elected assemblies, not necessarily based on an extensive franchise but at any rate representative of local opinion. At best they claimed to be akin to the House of Commons, a view often advanced during the revolutionary struggle. The Crown recognized that assemblies were necessary to encourage settlement, allay unrest or suspicion of tyranny, and to help towards prosperity.

In England, the Privy Council, with its Committee on Plantation Affairs, was the final court of judicial appeal in cases arising from the colonies. The Board of Trade was responsible for day to day supervision of affairs, especially civil matters. The Secretary of State for the Southern Department was the minister responsible for military organization. Generally, the Board of Trade showed little imagination or flexibility in dealing with a maturing society. It kept a traditional pattern and operated the system which it had inherited.

A royal governorship was no sinecure if the duties were to be effectively carried through. He was the leader of land and sea forces, was given the right to call or dissolve the assembly and was given:

full Power and Authority to make, constitute and ordain Laws, Statutes and Ordinances for the publick Peace, Welfare and good Government [provided that they were not] repugnant but as near as may be agreeable to the Laws and Statutes of this Our kingdom of Great Britain.

Judgment and discretion were called for, although in 1752 governors were ordered to obey instructions implicitly, a demand irregularly followed. Tact and diplomacy were needed to transmit orders of the Privy Council to assemblies, but all too rarely were such qualities evident in the men selected. In 1770 the *Public Advertiser* exclaimed:

Whenever we find ourselves encumbered with a needy Court-Dangler whom, on Account of Connections, we must not kick down Stairs, we kick him into an American Government.

At worst the governors might be described as 'fitter for a bedlam, or other hospital, than to be set over a respectable province'; or complaints made that they were 'generally entire Strangers to the People they are sent to govern . . . they seldom regard the Welfare of the People, otherwise than they can make it subservient to their own particular Interest'.

Usually the governors were dull and conventional, men little inclined to be thoughtful of the future if the present were comfortable enough. Their power was checked by the refusal of local assemblies to grant them permanent salaries and, more particularly, by their lack of patronage. There was no chance of a governor buying a band of faithful followers in key positions in the colony when London refused to grant a civil list. Gradually the powers of the governors declined, during the Seven Years' War at an alarming rate. In the event of rebellion they had inadequate coercive force at their disposal; outside the introduction of royal troops their power depended on the loyal affections of the people.

The councils likewise lost their way in the eighteenth century. Their function was to advise the governor, to be the highest court of local appeal and to check the popular assembly if need be. Merchants and planters sat in the councils, men often with divided loyalties who were singularly ineffectual in controlling the lower house.

The officials who completed the framework of government were concerned to implement government decisions. They were appointed in London in just the same way as men appointed for duty in Yorkshire. Judges of the Vice-Admiralty courts, customs officials, superintendents of Indian affairs, Treasury officials, officers and men stationed in Boston or Quebec, all were servants of the king, not of the local colony. In number they were few and like the governor and his council could hardly resist public violence.

The initiative which lay with the Houses of Assembly, called by various titles in different colonies, was immense. As the English had struggled under the Tudors and Stuarts towards more broadly based power, gaining victories despite numerous setbacks, so the Americans. Advantage was taken of the Seven Years' War to hold the government to ransom, so that the parallel between the Virginian House of Burgesses and the House of Commons was not so preposterous as it would seem to an Englishman like Squire Western, ignorant of the facts. For many years the procedure, privileges claimed, and sole control of financial affairs had been like the Commons. There had been no intervention to prevent accretion of power because it seemed hardly likely to affect the prosperity of the colonies, which was the most important consideration.

The franchise was hardly democratic, although the 40/- freehold qualification generally held. Women, Catholics, Jews, infidels, Negroes and indentured servants were debarred. Throughout the colonies, as a generalization, about one in four white males were eligible to vote, but of these only one in four exercised their right. This political apathy is hardly surprising in a fluid society. Rather more noteworthy democratically, was the opportunity for most men who wished to carve out political careers; the assemblies were effective arenas in which reputations could be made.

These assemblies were supported by publicity, not necessarily by favourable decisions, in the law courts. Common law in the eighteenth century continued to gain power as society became more complex. It protected property and also helped to develop the maturity of the nation through study of constitutional practice and the training which it afforded the radical thinker. In Massachusetts the rights of customs men to search for smuggled cargoes in 1760 was disputed and the case of Writs of Assistance was heard the following year. James Otis led the attack on the validity of such warrants, and by a piece of magnificent oratory impressed the learned as well as the popular mind with his belief that they were a denial of natural liberty. The official verdict upheld the Crown's rights but the writs could never be used effectively in Massachusetts again.

In Virginia the Two Penny Act, a regulation lowering the Anglican parson's salary which passed the House of Burgesses in 1758, was later declared void by the Privy Council. The clergy tried to recoup their back pay. In 1763 the Reverend James Maury sued the public for financial loss. After the court had admitted his claim but had not determined the amount of damages, a lawyer, Patrick Henry, made an impassioned address first denying the right of judges to set aside decisions of the House, and secondly haranguing the clergy as rapacious harpies. So effective was his pleading that Mr Maury received only one penny damages and Henry collected an enviable reputation.

There is no doubt that Americans enjoyed political discussion. In the states of New England this was still laced with theological implications but elsewhere the argument ran in a distinctive English vein continuing the whig traditions of John Locke and the Cato letters of Gordon and Trenchard. Support for the revolution of 1688 was universal; the opinions of Filmer and the Jacobites were discredited. Americans saw the liberty of the people enshrined in English constitutional forms, with the rights of the governors and the governed nicely balanced. They recognized the protection given to the individual and laid particular emphasis on freedom of the press, trial by jury and free elections. The participation of the people in the development of constitutional forms was deemed to be part of the natural order. The reverence shown towards the English heritage coupled with the belief that they had improved upon it is shown in an article of the *Boston Independent Advertiser* for 1749:

From this happy Constitution of our Mother Country, Ours in This is copied, or rather improved upon: Our invaluable CHARTER secures to us all the English Liberties, besides which we have some additional Privileges which the Common People there have not. Our Fathers had so severely felt, the Effects of Tyranny, and theWeight of the Bishop's Yoke, that they under went the greatest Difficulties and Toils, to secure to themselves, and transmit to their Posterity, these invaluable Blessings:– And we their Posterity are this Day reaping the Fruits of their Toils: – Happy, beyond Expression! in the Form of our Government – In the Liberty we enjoy – if we know Our own Happiness and know how to improve it.

That Americans believed themselves fully equipped with all the rights of Englishmen was a passionate undertaking. They felt that they possessed ultimate sovereignty in the form of the assembly. In opposing the power of parliament they acknowledged the supremacy of the Crown, but when the time was ripe they were prepared to jettison that, too. Their view of the empire was that it consisted of equal powers, under the Crown, forming a coordinated structure, but that any political body had the right to defend itself from arbitrary government.

Of equal importance in American political thought before 1763 was the doctrine of natural law, the ordinances for government laid down by God and realized by every man through intuition. The absence of definition led to ambiguity and contradictory interpretation, but eighteenth-century opinion was prepared to accept this irrational situation. Certainly the theologically conscious New Englanders appreciated Divine law most readily. In England Locke had stressed the natural law of property, the right to protect possessions and interests. Although he had written to defend the revolution of 1688 Locke's theory was used in the eighteenth century to maintain order in the mother country.

The whigs were concerned to protect themselves against Jacobite and tory, agreeing only to quarrel among themselves for the fruits of office. Merchants could use natural law to justify their pressure upon the government to keep the colonies in a subservient position; the capital tied up in America and her trade was considerable. Colonists and Englishmen used the same argument to defend their particular case. No wonder the ambiguities in this appeal led to utter confusion and misunderstanding.

Yet what had been the constitutional practice prior to 1763? The power of the Crown was not denied; in colonial disputes an appeal was often made to royal sovereignty. Similarly Parliament was seen to be increasingly important, legislation both internal and external being made for, and accepted by, the colonies without undue fuss. Certainly there was no effort made before 1763 to deny Parliament's right to legislate and the number of laws passed which related to colonial affairs was vast; the Navigation Act of 1696 stated that all laws passed in the colonies against it should be utterly void; the Post Office Act of 1710 and Paper Money Act of 1751 were not condemned as unconstitutional despite their sweeping interference. Lawyers and judges needed parliamentary statutes to support their cases, and despite inconsistencies the relevance of legislation was accepted as were the orders of the Privy Council, a body which refused to ratify colonial laws if they contravened an act of Parliament. More effort was made to evade laws than to deny their constitutional validity; the importance of the colonial intellectuals was to find a legal case to support the economic and emotional reasons for defiance. Precedents in strictly legal terms were unfavourable to the colonists, though they could appeal to those theorists of natural law – Aristotle and St Thomas Aquinas.

[5] SOCIAL AFFAIRS

In 1775 there were some 2½ million settlers in America, of whom ½ million were Negro. About 60 per cent were of English stock, and 14 per cent were Scots or Scots from Northern Ireland, usually called Scotch/Irish. The largest European group was the Germans with about 8 per cent. New Englanders were predominantly English as were the tidewater aristocrats of the South, but the presence of so many racial groups broke down the Old World's national distinctions. The English settlers also had no intention of allowing royal supremacy to swamp their prosperity or rigorously control their lives – after all, they or their ancestors had emigrated to avoid tutelage. Crèvecoeur's book *What is an American?*, published in 1782, almost idealizes these sturdy pioneers:

I respect them for what they have done, for the accuracy and wisdom with which they have settled their territory; for the decency of their manners; for their early love of letters; their ancient college [Harvard, founded in 1636], the first in this hemisphere; for their industry. . . . There never was a people . . . who with so ungrateful a soil have done more in so short a time.

From a survey of the colonies it is apparent that the development of America was determined by numerous factors which could conflict within a single colony. Social pressures had built up in North Carolina so that the Regulator risings of 1770, led by Presbyterian Scotch/Irish and Germans, reflected the ostracism of the upcountry settlers. This was the most serious protest against a colonial government before 1775. Merchants were often suspected by planters and the eastern farmers by the western pioneers. Old World class distinctions, however, were conspicuously absent. An American aristocrat was not one by European definition as there was no hereditary system. The opportunity to prosper was abundant and wealth, because everybody's money was new, created social opportunity. In the South the aristocrat, though living a stylish and European-conscious social whirl, was

hard working to sustain his property and family. Trade was regarded as a legitimate source of profit by landed men who had
no social prejudice against fortunes made in that manner.
William Byrd II of Westover, Virginia, is an excellent example of
an American landowner: he undertakes personal supervision of his
estates, is concerned with the investment of capital, is a medical
doctor to his family and slaves, a scholar (up at three in the
morning to read Hebrew, Greek or Latin until breakfast time),
gambler and occasional womanizer.

The hard work which was the basis of American prosperity
was also seen in towns, where the 'Protestant ethic' was married
to enterprise in so successful a fashion. New England provinces
saw a clear connection between godliness and wealth, impiety and
poverty. Certainly there were ample opportunities to work as
labour was at a premium. Fortunes were made from humble
beginnings – as for example the family of John Hancock, patriot
and signer of the Declaration of Independence. Nathaniel Hancock was a shoemaker in Boston and father of thirteen children;
his grandson was a merchant grandee and the grandson's heir
was the patriot John, who flouted the Navigation Acts.

The power of religious groups was still extensive in the eighteenth century. Respect for religion or the power of the preacher
was universal. The Church of England was established in the
southern colonies and in the four lower counties of New York.
In such areas local taxes paid the salary of the priest and, although
this was often resented, to be an Anglican was increasingly
fashionable. In Pennsylvania the Anglicans worked alongside the
Quakers and enjoyed power far exceeding their numerical
strength. Yet no bishop was appointed for America and priests
had to travel to England for ordination. Inevitably, the majority of Americans enjoyed the sacraments without the ceremony
of confirmation. The Bishop of London, who was responsible
for the spiritual life of his American flock, who called themselves Episcopalians, urged the government to appoint a bishop.
This was quite unacceptable to either the Cabinet or dissenters.
The former wished to consolidate greater power in London
rather than grant privileges which would accentuate the divi-

sions of the empire. The latter, growing numerous as immigration proceeded, loathed the implications of episcopacy which they equated with popery. Especially the Scotch/Irish, they depicted palaces, luxury and political tyranny as a natural corollary of an American bishop. They ignored the Anglican plea that a bishop was required to organize his own denomination, not to subvert the religious liberties of another. In the south the Society for the Propagation of the Gospel was strong, but Episcopalian belief was not seen to be the same as loyalty to England when trouble came. Fervent revolutionaries were to be found among southern Episcopalians, which was not often the case in the north.

The most momentous religious event in the eighteenth century was the Great Awakening. This followed the fiery oratory of a group of ministers the most prominent of whom were the Englishmen, George Whitefield, a follower of John Wesley, and Jonathan Edwards, a strict Calvinist in New England. Although by 1744 zeal was on the wane the effect of the movement was felt throughout the revolutionary period. Indeed the enthusiasm of the mobs for the Word of God was to be channelled towards political objectives in the 1760s, and the cause for freedom from sin expanded to include freedom from British tyranny. This dogmatic preaching certainly roused the Scottish Presbyterians against Britain and heightened Protestant consciousness. When the Quebec Act was passed in 1774 recognizing Roman Catholicism in that province, the government was branded as papist. Little wonder that Catholicism was the creed of very few and that Maryland, founded as a haven for persecuted Catholics, quickly came under the control of Episcopalians.

Negro slaves had first appeared in Virginia in 1619 but only slowly did they replace indentured servants, whites who had signed away their freedom and labour for a specified number of of years in return for a passage to the New World and a grant of land when their servitude was completed. Slavery was never legally instituted, but the status of the Negro was not seriously questioned before the War of Independence. Local laws rigorously controlled his activity, especially in South Carolina where the high percentage of slaves made insurrection possible. The passage from Africa was fraught with a high mortality rate, but the demand was constant and prices favourable, so the trade continued. The largest market existed in the southern states, though in the eighteenth century large gangs were uncommon – in the Upper South the average holding was eight to ten slaves; in South Carolina along the tidewater it was twenty-five to thirty. Even the Creek and Cherokee Indians kept Negro slaves.

The growth of the Negro population was swift. Children took the status of the mother, even though the father may have been white. Black society was essentially slave despite the free Negroes, manumitted by their owners perhaps for bravery or in a moment of conscience, but Negroes generally belonged to neither an African nor a white culture. The institution was encouraged for its economic importance. Georgia, for example, originally forbad slavery, but the government was forced by the planters' economic arguments to give way despite moral objections. Jefferson in Virginia loathed the institution and demanded freedom and transportation back to Africa for all Negroes, an idea which stimulated the settlement of Liberia in the mid-nineteenth century but which was only marginally successful. He could not, however, see the House of Burgesses accepting any such crippling scheme.

Originally redskinned Indians had inhabited the American continent. Families had come from Siberia via Alaska. By 1500 they numbered no more than a million in all. Their settlements had reached the Atlantic but with inadequate defences they were unable to prevent European colonization. In the south the Indians were generally disunited, over-partial to rum and relied upon the trader for clothes and firearms, all of which minimized their contribution to the War of Independence. Farther north, on the upper reaches of the Hudson River, the five tribes of the Iroquois nation made a more positive contribution to American society. In government they bequeathed ideas found later in the Constitution: for example, a union which was responsible for war and foreign affairs, but which did not interfere with the internal affairs of any tribe. Their legends and ritual also displayed great beauty. The British used the Iroquois against both the French in the Seven Years' War, and also against the colonial rebels in 1776.

Beyond the Appalachians the Indians soon became aware of the covetous nature of the American frontiersman; only government regulation preserved their possessions before 1775. After that date they found little mercy – even less after the War of 1812. Land was ruthlessly obtained by the pioneer farmer whose wasteful economy and growing numbers forced the frontier further west.

Social contact between Americans and Englishmen was minimal. By 1763 the feeling in London, prompted much by the opinion of regular army officers, was that the colonists were inferior people and their country belonged to Britain. On the one hand they were regarded as uncivilized, lacking those social accomplishments which made London a centre of art and manners; on the other they were seen as political inferiors. An unhealthy contempt was felt by the British for the foreign immigrant – 'a hotchpotch medley of enthusiastic madmen'. The American was a dependant and underestimated. The qualities of Benjamin Franklin were recognized by the political seers of London but John Bull was ignorant and prejudiced about American affairs; in 1763 he felt that the colonials should pay for their own defence and was prepared to brook no insubordination. Such an attitude remained until 1781.

However, this was to ignore the elements of sophistication apparent in much of American social life by the 1760s. Every region had local newspapers which both informed their readers about the outside world, and reflected their own points of view. Between 1763 and 1775 the number of newspapers doubled in the colonies. This growth was due partly to the political controversies, not least the Stamp Act which taxed newspapers and aligned the editors with both merchants and lawyers.

Culturally, the colonies were far from being an arid desert. Educational opportunity was expanding, and the colleges of Harvard, Yale and Princeton were already preeminent. Their religious foundations had gradually given way to more worldly concepts. Secondary schooling also grew apace, and only a few wealthy Americans sent their children to England to be educated. Private tutors and schools flourished, and free places multiplied, although among the poorer people education was often neglected, especially in the South. Even without much formal education Americans were often well read and articulate, most of all in the cities. Music was played and listened to; Charleston proudly boasted a St Cecilia Society, and an organ was to be found in many churches. Drama, too, was patronized, rather more freely in Virginia than in the North. The works of Shakespeare and the major English dramatists were performed by touring companies in makeshift theatres.

So, despite the absence of literary giants, and the frequency of borrowed tastes from England, the colonists were not nearly so ignorant as their brothers in Europe believed.

[6] ECONOMIC AFFAIRS

About 80 per cent of the colonists were concerned with agriculture and a further 10 per cent were engaged in allied occupations such as fishing or lumber. The cities were few and comparatively small; most Americans never visited the big eastern seaboard cities nor did they wish to. At the time of the Revolution the techniques employed by farmers were extremely simple; their success lay in the strength of their own hands and the clemency of the weather. This was an unremitting labour; to work the land and produce the necessities of life – houses, barns, tables and carts. It allowed of no rest and for the majority no prospect of wealth. At best the life was one of independence and contentment in which a man could improve his property and bring up a family, seeing growth resulting from his labour and passing on to his children more than he had himself received. There were few areas in Europe where such a life could be realized.

A mixed economy dominated the middle colonies. Wheat and cattle were exported in large quantities to the West Indies and

Europe. Farther south the staple crops were tobacco and rice, and in addition indigo, naval stores (turpentine, pitch, etc.), flax and hemp. Land was easily obtained in both areas which was an important social as well as economic factor. Richer plots were often reserved for the plantation owners or those who could pay officials for the privilege of first choice, but generally before the Revolution the amount of land was unlimited and there was little real need to invade Indian territory beyond the Appalachians. Men often wasted the soil, they disputed title deeds or were bitten with wanderlust but this could not disguise the fact that the ample supply of land catered for most men's needs. Some of the European ways of land-holding were introduced – primogeniture, the passage of property intact to the eldest son; or entail, the willing of property within a family for generations, were prominent south of New England – disappearing finally at the Revolution. These forms reduced the amount of land in circulation but were confined for the most part to the seaboard. In New England, although agriculture was not the source of greatest wealth, the authorities had established a system of landholding which was essentially equitable, so disputes were less frequent and society better ordered.

The pattern of trade throughout the Empire was governed by the Navigation Acts, the most obvious expression of a theory of protection or mercantilism. First passed in 1651 the acts were designed to secure English trade against the Dutch and their operation proved a source of wealth and power. Reaffirmed at the Restoration and later in 1696, the acts, supplemented by embargoes, bounties, tariffs, and treaties, regulated British trade up to 1775. Although modified where appropriate, they maintained the original intention of excluding foreign traders, building up naval manpower and making the empire self-sufficient. The provisions were: first, imperial ships alone could trade with the colonies; secondly, most goods either to or from the colonies had to pass through England and there arose the list of enumerated articles – tobacco, rice, tar, copper, iron, coffee and furs among others – whose exportation except through England was made illegal.

The theory was that each part of the British empire should contribute raw materials or industrial goods so that the whole could benefit from the diversity of the parts. By implication and in practice, Britain was the manufacturing partner, with North America engaged in agriculture and commerce permanently tied to a policy determined in London. Thus colonies were an integral part of the search for national wealth. They were expected to give of their natural resources and absorb the industrial article. According to John Campbell in 1772 an ideal colony is one where:

the inhabitants wear not a rag of their own manufacturing; drive not a nail of their own forging; eat not out of a platter or mug of their own making; nay . . . produce not even bread to eat.

Encouragement was given to the farmer and restrictions were laid on industrial capacity. The Iron Act of 1750 forbad colonists to erect any ironworks to process raw iron; the Hat Act of 1732 forbad the export of hats, thus protecting the London manufacturers. Neither act was effective. Legislation probably had less effect on the slow growth of industry than other factors such as the productivity of the soil, lack of capital, difficulty in marketing goods and high costs of labour. In such circumstances industry could offer a less stable reward than agriculture or commerce, although a prosperous section of the community was engaged in production. Their factories were small and manpower limited, though in 1748 a Swede wrote of Germantown, near Philadelphia:

Most of the inhabitants are manufacturers . . . in a short time this province will want very little from England.

Local laws in Pennsylvania, New Jersey and Massachusetts encouraged such activity, but they ran foul of the veto given by the Privy Council. But England was prepared in a small way to operate the laws against her own people at home; for example, tobacco growing was forbidden in the seventeenth century to help the prosperity of overseas plantations.

The balance of trade ran against the American colonies. Exports from Britain amounted to about £2 million per annum

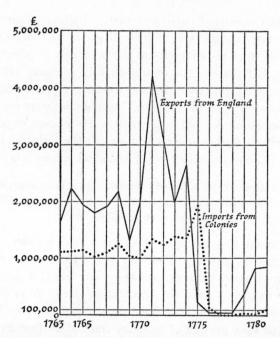

Statistics from: *Anderson*, Origin of Commerce *and Sheffield,*
Observations on Commerce

(*Extracted from D. M. Clark*, British Opinion and the American
Revolution [*Yale University Press*, 1930]; [*reissued Russell &
Russell*, 1966])

before 1768; thereafter the annual totals fluctuated as the political situation became less certain. About half of these goods went
to the southern colonies. Imports into Britain were between £1
million and £1½ million before 1774, two-thirds of this total
coming from the South. Despite their apparent wealth, many
American merchants and planters carried embarrassing burdens
of debt owed to London creditors. This was particularly true of
planters engaged in the production of tobacco, rice and indigo.
Although annual interest charges were regularly met in most
cases, Americans found immense difficulty in paying off the
capital sum.

Yet the hardship of the Navigation Acts was largely theoretical.

Both the cities of North America and the standard of living in the southern colonies reflected affluence even if this was built on credit facilities and smuggling. Trade through England proved beneficial in many ways: first, English manufactured articles were the best in the world; secondly, return cargoes from England were assured; thirdly, the opportunity to borrow money was available. In addition security was given by British troops against enemies. Even the often volatile anti-imperialist James Otis in 1764 declared:

The act of navigation is a good act, so are all that exclude foreign manufacturers from the plantation, and every honest man will readily subscribe to them.

This was a sentiment echoed by merchants in particular who, less interested in politics than in business, saw their prosperity founded on the British Empire. When the legislation of 1764 affected their position they sought for reform rather than rebellion, as would any other similarly threatened group.

PART II
Britain and America, 1756–70

[7] THE SEVEN YEARS' WAR 1756–63

The peace of Europe was re-established at Paris on 10 February 1763 and at Hubertusburg on 15 February. At the former Britain, France and Spain resolved their world-wide differences while at the latter Prussia, Austria and Saxony settled the German struggle, Russia having withdrawn from the conflict the previous year. In 1756 Frederick of Prussia had turned to Britain to prevent his complete isolation and when he attacked Saxony in August he and Pitt faced the rest of Europe. This was a 'diplomatic revolution'. The war on the continent fluctuated, was grisly in terms of both men and money, and until 1761 Prussian power ebbed away. Had Russia been more vigorous to support Austria, Frederick could have been decisively overcome. The accession in 1762 of Catherine II, who maintained a peace policy, isolated Austria instead, thus leading to the peace settlement.

Cooperation between Prussia and Britain had ceased in 1762. As the French war was nearly won and Bute feared that Frederick was embarking upon another campaign, the annual subsidy of £670,000 paid since 1758 was withdrawn. Looking for allies, Frederick turned to Russia so that from 1764 Britain was herself isolated, a situation which caused acute embarrassment in 1777 after the American victory at Saratoga.

Britain and France had been especially at loggerheads in North America. Because Pitt had a high regard for the personal qualities of Clive, affairs in India were left much to the control of the East India Company. The government bore the brunt of the

North American campaign, however. The capture of Louisburg on 26 July 1758 by General Amherst meant that strategic control of the mouth of the St Lawrence passed from the French; since Lake Ontario had been secured in the same year by the fall of Fort Frontenac, prospects for 1759 were hopeful. An advance along the St Lawrence was undertaken. The task of leading the expedition against Quebec was assigned to Major-General James Wolfe, an unorthodox military thinker, with a small army of some 4,000 men and a naval detachment under Admiral Saunders. Denied any element of surprise Wolfe was doubtful of success as the city was so adequately fortified, but his brilliant control of strategy and command led to the successful scaling of the Heights of Abraham on 13 September 1759 and the fall of Quebec five days later. The surrender of French possessions farther up the river confirmed British ascendancy, but it was not until the surrender of Montreal in September 1760 that Canada passed assuredly under British control. Thereafter the war in Europe had but little effect in North America.

What had been the attitude and the contribution of the American colonists to this war? Battle had been joined initially in the New World in 1754 when twenty-two-year-old George Washington, a lieutenant-colonel of the Virginia militia, fired on the French in the Ohio valley. General Braddock was sent from England in 1755, was defeated and killed, an event which, coupled with Admiral Boscawen's victory over a French convoy off North America in June, made official war certain. The colonists throughout the course of the war were often more interested in wresting political and economic power from the British government and their representatives than in fighting either the French or their allies, the Indians. There was a sad lack of cooperation. One colonial legislature refused to agree with another, except when both opposed the Crown; Maryland refused to join with Virginia in a military operation against the common enemy, and it also flooded the country with depreciated paper money. Its behaviour was intolerable and its citizens gained an unenviable reputation for republican ideals and unwarranted pride. Governor Horatio Sharpe complained that they were, 'Levellers

in their Principles and impatient of Rule . . . full of their own
opinions and entirely deaf to Arguments and Reason'. The
colonial assemblies employed similar tactics to those of the early
Stuart parliaments; they reckoned the grant of supplies to be conditional on the redress of grievances. Thus while the French swept
on they debated passionately the taxation of proprietary lands
(in Maryland), or parsons' salaries (in Virginia), or writs of assistance (in Massachusetts), or stubbornly refused to contribute
any aid at all unless they were personally threatened; Massachusetts, Connecticut, New York and New Jersey alone sent the
troops asked of the colonies. It was only after 1758 when the
colonies knew that the expense of the war would be carried by
Britain, and not by themselves, that they gained enthusiasm.

Although it may be possible to sympathize in part with
colonial resistance to British leadership, two other features are
very difficult to accept. The first is the failure of the colonists to
unite among themselves. In 1755 they rejected the Albany Plan
drawn up by Benjamin Franklin and accepted by the Albany
Congress of 1754 when representatives of seven colonies met to
discuss Indian problems and defence. The British government
was also opposed to the scheme, but vehement opposition arose
in America from legislatures which saw a threat to their personal
power. The difficulty of union was to plague the opposition to the
Crown for another twenty years.

The second feature was trading with the enemy. Throughout
the war there was a British blockade of French possessions where-
ever possible. This was consistently run by American ships which
had built up an extensive smuggling trade well before the war.
'The Saints of New England', especially those of Boston and
Rhode Island, were adept at respectable smuggling. The wealth
of the colonies depended upon this activity which was 'approved
by a robust public opinion but forbidden by parliamentary
statutes' (Arthur Schlesinger). During the war the trade was
extended and consequently prolonged French resistance. For
example, the French fleet in the West Indies was so well provi-
sioned that it was able to sail to the defence of Cape Breton and

frustrate the British attack on the island. A letter from New
England in the Newcastle papers states:

It is certain that the Inhabitants of Canada do at no time raise Pro-
visions sufficient to their Support, and that were it not for the great
Supplies thrown in from Several Neighbouring English Colonies . . .
the king [of France] could not maintain his Troops in that wretched
Country, so that these People in their Marches to Destroy one English
Province, are actually supported by the Bread raised in another.

Such trading occupied the attention of the British navy and
added to the burden of war. For the colonies it proved lucrative,
so small wonder that Massachusetts fought so strenuously against
the Writs of Assistance, British measures to restrain the trade
through search for, and seizure of, illicit cargoes.

Thus the burden of the war for the protection of the colonies
and the removal of French influences in North America was
maintained by British taxes, with the army and the navy of the
Crown. The regular officers despised the American troops. Wolfe
called them: 'the dirtiest, most contemptible cowardly dogs that
you can conceive'. Certainly there was a failure in human rela-
tionships here; the colonial resented the soldier and the soldier
underestimated the qualities of the colonial. This laid up trouble
for the future.

The American war had cost £60 million which contributed
greatly to the accumulated National Debt in 1763 of £140 million.
Now that the French threat had been removed, faced with this
unprecedented sum and noting the prosperity of the colonials, it
is hardly surprising that the government wished for a more
positive contribution from the colonies towards their own welfare.

[8] THE BRITISH GOVERNMENT

The extent of the British Empire in 1763 owed much to the vision of men like William Pitt. The Peace of Paris was a vindication of his imperial policy, although he believed the terms would have been more favourable had he retained office. Yet through war Britain was undisputed master of the world's trade. In North America she had gained all Canada and Cape Breton Island and from Spain she took Florida. Spain was given Louisiana, the vast area to the west of the Mississippi, by France as compensation, so it was apparent that French ambitions on the mainland had been finally disappointed. In the West Indies Britain took Grenada, Dominica, St Vincent and Tobago; in Africa, Senegal; in India she retained all her conquests over native rulers in Bengal and British influence elsewhere predominated, although the situation territorially between France and the East India Company was that of 1749.

Pitt objected to the many concessions allowed the French. He deplored the recognition of their fishing rights off Newfoundland and in the Gulf of the St Lawrence, and the possession there of two small islands. He bitterly opposed the settlement in the West Indies, which returned to them the sugar islands, potential centres of military advantage, and in Africa. The government had not smashed French power completely but had left her as a threat to merchant interests. The settlement had not been harsh enough for him; 'We have given her [France] the means of recovering her prodigious losses and becoming once more formidable to us at sea'. Lord Bute, the leader of the government, preferred the path of moderation and the maintenance of France as a great power. The French, far from being grateful for this respite, struck at British power at the first opportunity, as Pitt had prophesied.

This empire had to be administered. The acquisition of Canada meant that Britain was responsible for vast areas of land, including that to the south of Canada between the Appalachian mountains and the Mississippi, largely unproductive and with a potentially hostile Indian population as Pontiac's rebellion in 1763 showed. The government was forced to consider financial problems which had become acute during the war itself as well as future planning. The Board of Trade and Plantations was asked to report on problems of government, policing and colonial contribution towards payment for the security and development of the area. Grenville's ministry inherited a mammoth problem which should not be underestimated.

British governments in the period 1763-75 were unable to bring to colonial affairs that perception which was required. Sharing in the general ignorance of things American, both Crown and ministers failed to adopt a sound and consistent policy. Domestic politics took priority and the bold schemes adopted in colonial matters were withdrawn only after their failure had created permanent harm to the relationship between mother country and her subjects. Even the Coercive Acts were modified in 1775, but too late to be effective.

The rigidity of the political views of George III did not assist a solution to these problems. The king, antagonistic towards professional politicians and anxious that his opinions should count in the affairs of state, sought ministers who would reflect his ideas. Lord Bute was politically savaged and resigned in 1763. George Grenville was altogether stronger. He was a business man with a reputation for financial skill. Itching to deal with the vast debt accumulated during the war, he sought retrenchment if not reform. Chatham (Pitt) and his ministry of 1766 seemed to rise above party and to be in sympathy with royal principles which distrusted loyalty to any other than the Crown. Chatham believed that American grievances were justified, but his position in the House of Lords rather than the Commons, and the deterioration in his mental condition meant that he exercised inadequate control over his colleagues, Townshend in particular. During his ministry, and that of Grafton, the colonial problems became more acute.

George III found his most congenial leader in Lord North, who was 37 when he became chief minister. He brought no great qualities or policies to his ministry in 1770; perhaps this was just as well, because the sixties had been littered with strong men or ideas, and government had proved well nigh impossible. The success of North lay in his ability to conciliate and prove acceptable to both king and Commons. Had it not been for the American issue, actually dormant between 1770 and 1773, he might have succeeded as had Walpole. He sat in the Commons himself and was an accomplished speaker, although not so much an orator as a tactician; he showed consummate skill in playing one minister off against another yet remaining acceptable to them both. He did bring to government a widely accepted flair for finance (the younger Pitt later expanded his work in this field). The incidence of land tax was kept at three shillings in the pound during 1772–4, which gave him popularity with the independent members of Parliament though he did sacrifice military and naval expenditure, a policy which later had disastrous effects. His solution of the East India Company crisis, as shown by the Regulating Acts of 1773, was highly acceptable to the Commons and tactfully sold to the directors. So successful was he that Chatham writing to Shelburne in 1774 said:

He serves the Crown more successfully and more sufficiently, upon the whole, than any other man now to be found could do.

He suffered a nervous breakdown in 1778, and broken in spirit and policy, wishing to admit defeat but not daring to communicate these ideas to the king, or resign, or change his tactics, he stayed put doing little until all was lost in 1782.

Some ministers and M.P.s were sympathetic to the North Americans. However, among the senior statesmen only Pitt can be described as a staunch friend. Although he had little specialist knowledge of American politics, he was prepared to argue that it was neither lawful nor expedient that the colonies should be taxed. He rejoiced that the Stamp Act had been resisted because he feared the arbitrary power of government as Bute and George III were believed to exercise it. Yet he was a mercantilist and saw the colonies as a source of profit for Britain, accepting taxation as a means of regulating trade, not as a means of raising revenue. Also, he accepted that ultimate sovereignty must be

reserved to Britain and for her to lose her colonies would be a
death blow. His last speech in the House of Lords, in 1778, deplored the suggestion that America should be allowed independence. But before the conflict broke out his reaction to American
aggression was not to demand reprisals but, as in 1774, after the
Boston Tea Party, to seek reconciliation to prevent a war which
Britain could only lose. In 1775 he issued his 'Plan for Settling
the Troubles in America', but he was two years too late. He was
supported in many of these ideas by Edmund Burke, Lord Shelburne and Charles James Fox but they were never a sizeable
minority.

After the election of 1761 there were 558 members of Parliament for 315 constituences. Only 48 of these constituences had
been contested, for the most part by a severely restricted elector-
ate. The results Namier calls 'remarkably normal'. It was this
Parliament which, under the terms of the Septennial Act, lasted
until 1768 and was responsible for the passage of the Sugar and
Stamp Acts and the Townshend duties. All the authorities on
American affairs during the next fifteen years had entered the
House by 1768, all at by-elections; Lieutenant-Colonel Isaac
Barré, who had served in America; Richard Jackson, agent in
England for the state of Connecticut; Edmund Burke, agent for
New York 1770-4; Thomas Pownall, governor of Massachusetts
1757-60 – these were among the most prominent. Five Americans,
all northerners, sat in the House between 1763 and 1783; no
southerner sat, probably because as landowners they preferred
their own country and were not so wealthy as northern merchants.
Americans sat for London and Bristol only after the relationship with the colonies had begun to deteriorate; in Bristol the
American extraction of the candidate, Cruger, was made an
election issue, but he still won. In general, however, it can be
seen that America lacked representation through native born
and bred members.

There were groups of men in the House of Commons who had
intimate connections with America. First, there were the West
Indians; 13 in the Parliament of 1761 had been born in the islands
and held office there. In addition there were eight or nine who

had West Indian connections. Yet Americans distrusted West Indians in London and with good reason because their interests, especially sugar, often clashed. On constitutional issues the West Indians, of whom Beckford was the most important, voted against the ministry, for example opposing the Stamp Act in 1765, a measure which was carried by 245 to 49 votes.

Second, there were the merchant members of Parliament; ten of these, although they had never travelled to America, were well informed and corresponded regularly with the colonies. On matters which did not adversely affect their own trading interests they supported the American cause, advised by colonial agents in London. One example of this combined power was the reshaping of the Mutiny Bill in 1765, which contained clauses to billet soldiers in private homes, so that it became a far less oppressive measure. The industrialization of England weakened merchant influence and by 1775 they were no longer a powerful lobby.

Third, the 59 army officers returned in 1761 included six who had been to America, four of whom still held commands there. The most faithful to the American cause was Isaac Barré, an untypical officer, who had been debarred from promotion because he lacked breeding and connections. He sympathized with the aspirations of the colonists against the pretensions of British overlords. The officers generally did not share this view; for example 23 of them voted against the repeal of the Stamp Act, a high percentage. Of the 21 naval officers probably the majority had been to America and realized its strategic value.

Finally, there were the land speculators, among them merchants, officers, lords and ministers. They had secured grants of land in America and were involved in maintaining their property.

Few of these men were trusted by the Americans and they could not be called representatives of colonial opinion. Self-interest dominated their thoughts and the vast majority did not discern the radical nature of local assemblies and their influence in the colonies. They were bound by mercantilist principles but were never a united opposition to government measures. The passage of the Sugar and Stamp Acts was virtually unopposed and later support for the colonials centred on Chatham and Burke rather than upon those with first-hand experience of overseas conditions.

One source of extra-parliamentary influence on the government was the colonial agent. Only a few of them were members of Parliament. Their task was to present the colonial argument to whoever in London was concerned in decisions relating to their colony. Merchants, Privy Councillors or ministers were advised or reproached by them, and they wrote pamphlets. Assemblies in America issued instructions and received information from men as eminent as Franklin, who strove valiantly to create an ideal public image. Some Englishmen looked upon the agents as accredited representatives of the colonies, protesting that the Americans did not need members of Parliament in addition. But only eight colonies by 1775 employed agents and their advice was so obviously ignored, or their influence so limited in England, that their presence rather indicated the futility of American representations and undermined ideas of a federation.

British government in the second half of the eighteenth century was highly respected in Europe as was the healthy intellectual and cultural life of her people. This was the nation of David Hume, the Scottish philosopher, and Edward Gibbon, the historian; of the writers Dr Johnson, Oliver Goldsmith and Richard Brinsley Sheridan; of Sir Joshua Reynolds and Gainsborough in portrait painting; of classical elegance in architecture by James Gibb, and in furniture by Chippendale and Hepplewhite; of the scientists Cavendish and Priestley. Although her politicians may have been less than brilliant this assemblage showed a high degree of civilization; the Americans, however, were more involved in their own domestic affairs and could not afford to display respect for a tutelage which was becoming rapidly more irksome.

[9] GRENVILLE: PROCLAMATION, SUGAR AND STAMPS

The major problem which emerged from the Peace of Paris was the future of Canada, the area along the St Lawrence river, and the vast tract of land west of the Appalachians but east of the Mississippi. To all intents and purposes it was either a barren land or unexplored, certainly without immediate mercantile advantage. It was populated by Indians, a potential enemy brought into greater prominence when the French threat had been eliminated. The cost of policing the area was too great for Grenville's ministry to contemplate seriously; as yet the notion of imperial grandeur in sheer acreage of territory was barely realized, nor could Grenville agree to a policy of American expansion which would cost the British taxpayer further exorbitant sums. Nor did he see the Americans themselves paying for the maintenance of armed forces in the hinterland; most influential Americans were concerned with trade or agriculture within the eastern seaboard belt. Internal political squabbles in individual colonies had shown that the assemblies lacked sympathy for the aspirations of the farmers and pioneers of the interior.

The Indian problem flared up in Pontiac's rebellion of May, 1763. He was the war chief of the Ottawa confederacy centred on Detroit and the rising was so successful initially that all British posts in the West were captured, except Fort Pitt and Detroit itself. Fear for the future was largely responsible for the rising; Englishmen had replaced the French at the centres of trade and the substitution caused dismay among the Indians. Whereas the French had given lavishly to their allies and had included the Indians in their empire, the British withdrew from bribery, became exclusive and believed that the Indians had outlived their usefulness. General Amherst was often tactless in his treatment of them. In the course of the war he even suggested that blankets infested with smallpox should be distributed. Others were sure that bloodhounds or rum would solve the problem. These attitudes were shared by frontiersmen and contrasted vividly with the

French concern for cooperation with the tribes. The new trappers were openly greedy and dishonest, despising the Indian and his culture. Thus this rising was an attempt to reverse the military decisions of 1759 and 1760.

Indian success was widespread; garrisons were surprised and murdered. At one fort where whites were watching a game of lacrosse between two tribes, the teams' enthusiasm turned to war whoops, sticks were dropped and weapons produced, with the result that sixteen soldiers were killed and the rest captured without retaliation. The rules of warfare were Indian based. Captive whites became slaves, or were tortured, for example Lieutenant Gordon who was roasted over a slow fire for several nights before he died, and corpses were mutilated. Amherst moved slowly at first, but when he gathered momentum the rising was already on the wane. Pontiac had hoped for help from Louis XV, but when news came of the Peace of Paris he realized the isolation of his people. Indian war confederacies were notoriously difficult to sustain and after the first significant British victory at Bushy Run in August 1763, the allies began to disintegrate. It was not until 1765 that Pontiac smoked the pipe of peace and recognized George III as his father. From this war the government learnt how to handle Indians; brutality and disdain gave way to conciliation and care so that by 1812 the Indians were prepared to fight for the British against the American 'war hawks'.

During the initial panic of 1763 the ministry rushed through the Proclamation Act as a temporary measure. Until 1775 it remained a source of grievance because it was never modified to meet new situations, although British policy was often inconsistent. The boundary line drawn approximately along the high ridge of the Appalachians to prevent immediate confrontation between the white man and Indian became a stifling measure. No British subject could settle west of this line, a serious bar to expansion. The intention was not to exclude the trader, or to cramp the colonies indefinitely, but to prevent war and military expenditure. Despite the administration of Johnson and Stuart, two able and shrewd commissioners appointed by the Crown to take charge of Indian relations, the government could not raise revenue sufficient to buy the Indian hunting grounds and thus solve the problem of white settlements. In the absence of any lead the frontiersmen took the law into their own hands and moved west, even the governor of Virginia making grants of land beyond the 1763 demarcation line.

By 1776 a growing white community in Kentucky showed the failure of the Proclamation Act. The government could protect neither the Indian nor the white settler through its inadequate chain of forts, so failing to maintain the initiative in the west. An alternative plan to divert expansion to the north and south never succeeded. Nova Scotia and Florida were more easily defended and their contribution to imperial wealth more highly regarded, but the movement of expansion remained through the middle colonies. In fact the government was trying to alter an already apparent trend in American society, westward economic expansion. The wasteful nature of American farming was seen most clearly in tobacco which exhausted the soil in seven years, but generally farmers exploited new lands rather than worked the old scientifically. A growing population demanded more land, but royal prohibitions, not only beyond the Appalachians but also in 1773 preventing further grants of crown lands within the established colonies, brought movement to a snail's pace causing frustration and anger. Although by 1775 the government was willing to abolish the demarcation line, this was not made apparent to the colonists.

Important though the problem of the western lands was, the most explosive area lay in the east, along the seaboard, and concerned the more sophisticated and cosmopolitan urban population. It was here that Grenville's reorganization of the financial system was most keenly felt. The need for reshaping the economy was apparent and could not be ignored. In the circumstances it was the government's duty to make the existing machinery of trade regulation more efficient, to improve customs, and to create a revenue which would remove the colonies, with its standing army, as an expense on the British taxpayer. There was no intention of making Americans pay for the Seven Years' War, but rather to share the burden of peacetime finance. The belief that this was an attempt to destroy colonial freedom or to exercise an unwarranted tyranny is difficult to sustain; it is unnecessary to read into the changes a distinctively 'tory' approach. The reasonableness of Grenville's legislation was accepted by all shades of political opinion in England, the opposition in America being the result of understandable self-interest during an increasingly difficult period of trade.

In the process of legislation obvious departures were made from the practice of the past forty years. The Sugar Act was the first piece of legislation designed deliberately to raise a revenue in America. This intention differentiated it from other mercantile legislation which dealt only with the regulation of trade. The Stamp Act brought parliamentary taxation of internal affairs in the colonies, and the Quartering, or Mutiny, Act made them provide for troops in time of peace. The disputes dragged on, partly through the limitations imposed by distance, partly through lack of understanding, or political squabbles and jealousies in England which gave time for seeds of revolution to be sown. It may be argued that the colonies were already lost by 1770 and that the events of 1773-5 merely confirmed the maturity of the colonists in their political thought. Grenville however, did not rush his initial reforms and was prepared to abolish the proposed Stamp bill if a better solution could be offered. None was. Later there was an absence of pliability in British thinking towards the thirteen colonies. This contrasts most markedly with the concessions made to the Catholic French in Quebec in 1774. Without the willingness to concede change, a British victory in the war of 1775-83 would have been inevitably shortlived.

The Revenue Act of 1764 was sensibly conceived. It is often called the Sugar Act as some of the important clauses dealt with sugar and its by-products, molasses and rum. The 1733 Molasses Act had placed an import tax of sixpence a gallon on molasses, ninepence a gallon on rum and five shillings a hundredweight on sugar imported from foreign possessions. This was designed to protect the West Indian planters whose products were more costly than those of the French islands which had a vast surplus.

Although the French government aided their planters, it refused to allow rum into France for fear that brandy sales would be affected detrimentally. The incidence of smuggling into North America and open flouting of the act was acknowledged. The 1764 act reduced the molasses duty to threepence, forbad the importation of rum and raised the sugar payment to twenty-seven shillings. This made the duty on molasses most reasonable and gave protection to the rum distillers from foreign competition; in addition high duties were levied on many other foreign imports, indicating that the House of Commons seemed anxious to stimulate the American economy.

Further, the act attempted to strengthen the customs service to make these new regulations effective. Part of the difficulty lay in the corrupt nature of customs men, many of them absentees in England and paying deputies to act for them in the colonies. Others were on the spot to collect bribes or otherwise improve their lot. Grenville's act demanded that they all take up their posts, that the Royal Navy be empowered to help enforce the trade laws, and that Admiralty courts be enlarged. In particular, the merchants were more at the mercy of the Admiralty judge in Halifax, Nova Scotia, which meant far less chance of an acquittal than from a local court and jury. The price of being caught running the gauntlet of trade restrictions was now so costly that merchants were naturally afraid of the economic consequences.

Grenville hoped that not only would the customs service pay for itself (which it had not done previously) but that the revenue should help, according to the act, towards:

defraying the necessary expenses of defending, protecting, and securing the British colonies and plantations in America.

£45,000 per annum was expected, although this proved far too optimistic. It met only a small part of the cost of the army, but was important in persuading Englishmen that the government intended to broaden the basis of taxation. At home Grenville could not lower the land tax despite his pruning of expenditure. Various unpopular taxes were continued or introduced in England, so this Revenue Act was generally applauded.

At first the American merchants believed that the act was an attempt by the West Indian interests to undermine the economy. Slowly they turned to resent the act as a deliberate move to raise revenue rather than regulate trade, and thus to be contrary to the purpose of navigation laws. Yet their opposition was not whole-hearted. New England was far more disturbed than the southern plantations, and many Americans felt that when the act was seen to be detrimental to the life of New England it would be withdrawn in the interests of the empire as a whole. Men such as the smuggler Stephen Hopkins believed that England was killing the hen which laid her the Golden Egg.

Undoubtedly a trade recession was apparent in the North. This had been noticeable before the act but was accentuated by the new regulations. War had proved profitable for the merchants and they ran into a depression consequent upon peace. The chain of bankruptcies in New England testified to the evil nature of the times; in Pennsylvania it was said that:

Trade is become dull, Money very scarce, Contracts decrease, Lawsuits increase . . .

and again:

What is your city without Trade, and what the Country without a Market to vend their Commodities?

One means of protest was to cut the importation of luxury goods from England and attempt to be more self-sufficient – in Boston merchants gave up expensive mourning dress for funerals and workmen used Massachusetts leather for their clothes; home industries in linen and cloth flourished as part of the protest. Yet no one denied the constitutional legality of the act or denied the right of parliament to tax the colonies.

Also in 1764 Grenville passed his Currency Act. During the war paper money had circulated without undue control. After the war English merchants demanded that further issues of paper money should be made illegal so that debts could be fairly paid at face value. This was now done. Bills of credit tended to depreciate if indiscriminate printing was allowed, but in several colonies the banking had been efficient and the prohibition was regarded as a restriction on trade. This was an irritant on top of other British acts; although in 1773 all except the New England colonies were allowed to issue notes, the relaxation did not help to placate public opinion as had been hoped.

Before the full effect of the Sugar or Currency Act could be assessed, Parliament passed the Stamp Act in 1765. Stamp duties ranging from a halfpenny to £10, to be paid in coin and not by notes, were demanded on commercial papers (especially cargo shipments), legal documents (including tavern licences), pamphlets, newspapers and advertisements. The act had operated in England since 1694 and brought in £290,000 in 1760; in America it was calculated to raise £60,000 per annum to help defray the cost of the army, which was estimated at £350,000. The beauty of the procedure was that collection cost a minimal sum. There was no searching by a horde of officials; stamps had to be bought by the customer to legalize his documents. It was also an equitable tax which would be paid by all, not just one section of the community. Opposition to the bill in the House of Commons was negligible, and Grenville regarded it as complementary to his Sugar Act and part of the comprehensive plan of financial reform. He did not wish to antagonize the colonies and so he had conferred with their agents in London. They had been unable to suggest an alternative form of taxation and the minister felt confident in presenting the bill that American cooperation would be forthcoming. Both he and the agents seriously underestimated the decline in American prosperity and the resentment already caused by earlier legislation.

A large financial concession was made by Grenville when he appointed Americans as stamp masters, posts which carried patronage and which Benjamin Franklin was quick to seize for his friends. The comparative enthusiasm of the agents contrasted with the violent agitation with which the act was received in America. Jared Ingersoll, agent for Connecticut, wrote a very level-headed account of the parliamentary debate to Governor Fitch, ending:

What the event of these things will be I don't know, but am pretty certain that wisdom will be proper and even very necessary, as well as prudence and good discretion to direct the councils of America.

He was happy enough to accept a stamp mastership, a post which he swiftly relinquished.

Opposition to the Stamp Act was more pronounced than earlier protests because its provisions affected not only a far wider range of trades and professions, but also the more articulate members of the community. Tavern keepers, lawyers, newspapermen and merchants all feared for their livelihood. The unity of the professions was equalled by the geographical unity of northern and southern colonies, a feature conspicuously absent hitherto.

Popular feeling was expressed in many frightening ways. Stamp masters were an obvious target for mob violence. They were not only burnt in effigy, but their windows were broken and houses fired. The effectiveness of such action was undoubted and by 1 November 1765, when the act should have become operative, all the stamp agents had resigned. Not only those intimately concerned with the Stamp Act suffered. Governor Bernard wrote to the Earl of Halifax:

Everything that for years past had been the cause of any popular discontent was revived and private resentments against persons in office worked themselves in and endeavoured to execute themselves under the mask of the public cause.

An excellent example of this was the destruction of the house in Boston of the Lieutenant-Governor of Massachusetts, Thomas Hutchinson, an enemy of popular leaders:

As soon as the mob had got into the house, with a most irresistible fury they immediately looked about for him to murder him, and even made diligent enquiry whither he was gone. They went to work with a rage scarce to be exemplified by the most savage people. Everything moveable was destroyed in the most minute manner except such things of value as were worth carrying off, among which was near 1,000 pounds sterling in specie, besides a great quantity of family plate, etc. But the loss to be most lamented is that there was in one room . . . a large and valuable collection of manuscripts and original papers which he had been gathering all his lifetime and to which all persons who had been in possession of valuable papers of a public kind had been contributing as to a public museum . . . the loss to the public is great and irretrievable.

The structure of the house itself was too solid to be destroyed completely although the mob worked all night. That the rioting was not as spontaneous as appeared led William Bull in South Carolina to remark:

Although these very numerous assemblies of the people bore the appearance of common populace, yet there is great reason to apprehend they were animated and encouraged by some considerable men who stood behind the curtain.

Mob leadership was most usually vested in the Sons of Liberty, a radical organization which came into being first in Connecticut. It was a movement which the Governor of Georgia condemned as one 'such as to strike at the sovereignty of Great Britain'. This was the first effective movement of popular disapproval and later developed, by fits and starts, into the Continental Congresses of the 1770s. The impetus came from the wealthy: from John Scott of New York, lawyer graduate from Yale and a landowner; from John Hancock, merchant of Boston; and from Christopher Gadsden, merchant in South Carolina. They were responsible for the coordination and effectiveness of mob violence specifically designed to prevent the implementation of the Stamp Act by attacking the property, if not the persons, of the stamp masters. Oliver of Massachusetts, Coxe of New Jersey, Hood of Maryland and Mercer of Virginia were all terrorized into relinquishing their power.

A further objective of the rioters was the stock of stamps waiting to be issued on 1 November. The governors could not entrust them to the local militia so kept them on naval craft below decks, or in military fortresses, as happened in South Carolina at Fort Johnson. The fort fell to the Sons of Liberty when the garrison refused to offer any resistance. On the heels of such successes the Sons demanded that business and law should continue normally without stamps. At this, the movement began to fall apart because the property owners and political moderates took fright and feared the rule of 'mobocracy'. Judges often refused to operate their courts and were supported increasingly by merchant opinion. The repeal of the Stamp Act was reckoned by many to have saved authority in the colonies. For a different reason the Sons of Liberty also rejoiced at the repeal and the celebrations went far into the night; a ball in Virginia, fireworks in Connecticut (where a large number of patriots were killed when some gunpowder exploded accidentally), or just plain tavern drinking. The organization remained intact, though now with neither the desire nor the opportunity to be so active.

While the mob was busy protesting against the Stamp Act the local Assemblies were also agitated. Many had sent petitions to the House of Commons between the summer of 1764 and March 1765 to warn of the effect the act would have. The Commons refused to consider these petitions seriously and relied on their own judgment. Trouble flared up in the Virginia House of Burgesses on 30 May when Patrick Henry rose to speak. Although his exact words are a subject of dispute it would appear that he expected George III to profit from the example of Julius Caesar and Charles I, a declaration which the House thought to smack of treason. Following this blunt statement on the following day Henry introduced resolutions which stated the freedom of colonists to tax themselves, or consent to taxation, and that they should never be forced to give up the rights of free Englishmen. His final resolutions were the most dogmatic, including the belief that:

The inhabitants of this colony are not bound to yield obedience to any law . . . designed to impose any taxation whatsoever upon them . . . other than the laws of the General Assembly.

This was too much for his colleagues, and they refused to accept the radical proposals. It was hardly surprising that the Lieutenant-Governor dissolved the house the following day. Enough damage had been done.

The most statesmanlike move was the call for a congress to

consider the Stamp Act. Massachusetts asked the colonial legislatures to appoint delegates to meet in New York on 7 October 1765; nine colonies sent twenty-seven men, New Hampshire, Virginia, North Carolina and Georgia declining to do so. The congress was essentially a conservative body and the declaration published on 19 October reflects a desire to conciliate and expound rather than inflame and excite. Loyalty to parliament was acknowledged and the admission made that:

The people of these colonies are not, and from their local circumstances, cannot be represented in the House of Commons.

Yet the colonies alone might tax themselves. The Stamp and other Revenue Acts were attacked as possessing a 'manifest tendency to subvert the rights and liberties of the colonists'. They were undermining the economy, not only of the colonies, but of Great Britain herself. In this way an economic argument was added to the constitutional. The radicals, such as James Otis, were outvoted by the moderates, but Parliament ignored the petitions sent to it from the congress. Even in America the debates of these intellectuals were not given much public attention and the limelight rested on the activity of the mobs.

A boycott of British goods was organized, an extension of the protest which had followed the Sugar Act. In September 1765 the *New York Gazette and Post Boy*, followed later by the *Connecticut Gazette*, argued that Americans should abstain from the use of British articles until the Revenue Acts were repealed. Retailers in New York agreed to stop trade with Great Britain after 1 January 1766, while merchants instituted an embargo on European goods. When the Americans rallied to this form of protest orders in England fell off alarmingly. Certain vital goods, such as tackle for the fisheries, were still purchased, but the whole-hearted manner in which the boycott was enforced in ports where it had been accepted, brought a reaction across the Atlantic.

British merchants whose business was threatened with ruin by either the failure of trade (William Reeve of Bristol reported total stagnation), or a possible repudiation of debts by colonials, drew up petitions to the House of Commons. They pleaded for a

review of the Revenue Acts on economic and not constitutional
grounds. Their evidence was supported by Benjamin Franklin
who addressed the whole House on 28 January 1766. He explained the difference which colonists drew between external and
internal taxation; also he showed that Americans regarded the
war of 1754–63 not as one caused primarily by the demands of
the colonies, but rather as a struggle for European power between France and His Majesty's government, a piece of reinter-
pretation not generally acceptable in London.

Parliament was divided by the revenue issue; the Duke of
Bedford, Grenville and their followers were in favour of coercion,
of the destruction of charters and the dispatch of an army to
show that violence could not be used with impunity against servants of the Crown. They argued that to concede to the demands
of the mob was to display weakness which could only lead to further disturbances. However, Grenville and his ministry had been
dismissed in July 1765 and the new administration of Lord
Rockingham, Newcastle and Conway was more moderate and
with royal support had decided on repeal. Pitt supported the
government view and welcomed the opposition of the American
people to an intolerable law. He asked the House to repeal the
Stamp Act 'absolutely, totally and immediately' in the interests
of justice and equity. Lord Camden was even more dogmatic and
believed that 'taxation and representation are inseparably united',
despite the Stamp Act Congress resolve that representation was
impractical. In the Commons the debate was sharp and the
moderate view prevailed by only thirty-four votes. This solution
showed that in both England and America the economic issues
were of paramount importance.

The repeal of the Stamp Act in March 1766 was followed in
June by a new Revenue Act which considerably modified the
Sugar Act. Duties were reduced from threepence a gallon on
foreign molasses to one penny levied on all molasses imported
into the colonies from British or foreign sources. This made smuggling unprofitable and the duty raised in the colonies by the act
was the largest of any parliamentary act. The cash, now raised
without protest, was spent in the defence of America.

Yet also in March Parliament had passed the Declaratory Act stating that it:

hath, and of right ought to have, full power and authority to make laws and statutes of sufficient force and validity to bind the colonies and people of America, subjects of the Crown of Great Britain, in all cases whatsoever.

Pitt disapproved of the act as contrary to the distinction between external and internal taxation, but he was one of a tiny minority. For Englishmen this act was as important as the repeal of the Stamp Act, but the Americans, in their enthusiasm for the latter, failed to consider closely enough its implications. Their acceptance of the act adds weight to the argument that the Americans used the constitutional issue to support an essentially economic cause. What worried Americans was not the power of Parliament as such, but the prosperity of their people.

[10] THE TOWNSHEND DUTIES AND THEIR REPEAL

The Sons of Liberty believed they had forced the government to capitulate. This bred a spirit of insolence in the colonies towards the English and any movement to control trade or raise taxation in future was likely to be resisted by the rabble if not by property holders. Grenville's acts had failed and he had been pushed from office in 1765, for reasons unconnected with American affairs. The inexperienced Rockingham had been faced with the consequences of Grenville's legislation. His solution of moderation and withdrawal proved unattractive to the politicians because it seemed to accept the influence and pressure of rioters far too easily. In August 1766 therefore, Rockingham fell from power to be replaced by the Great Commoner, William Pitt, who in July had been created Earl of Chatham. His acceptance of a peerage dismayed many of his followers especially because it entailed his

removal to the House of Lords and allowed Charles Townshend
a comparatively free hand in the Commons. Chatham treated
his colleagues like children, and was utterly unreasonable. He
expected to be obeyed without question and his admiration for
the king was unbounded, a product of his mental instability. His
popularity declined within the Cabinet and outside, especially
in America where his obvious pleasure in taking a title was regarded with deep suspicion.

The ministry included men of all political persuasions, a deliberate experiment, which was expected to rescue government
from the evils of faction and to prevent liberty from degenerating
into licentiousness. Of the king's friends, North and Egmont were
included; of the friends of Chatham, Lord Shelburne was the most
outstanding, though probably the most disliked and distrusted.
He was Secretary of State for the Southern Department and the
colonies were within his jurisdiction. His plan for America envisaged the withdrawal of the 1763 line of demarcation along the
Appalachians and the removal of troops and officials in the west.
From three centres at Detroit, on the Illinois, and the lower
Mississippi the area was to be colonized by free enterprise with
minimal government aid. This was expected to create new opportunities for American initiative, lower the cost of military and
civil government considerably and restore harmony between
Britain and the old established colonies. Shelburne's scheme was
rejected, and the government turned instead to the measures
proposed by Townshend, Chancellor of the Exchequer.

It is extraordinary that a Cabinet so pro-American could have
accepted the Townshend duties, which were a return to Grenville's policy. Part of the trouble lay in the physical collapse of
Chatham in December 1766. For the next two years he lost control of policy and colleagues. Grafton, the First Lord of the Treasury, saw him in May 1767 with his 'nerves and spirits affected to
a dreadful degree and his great mind bowed down'. In 1768 he
gathered strength enough to resign and look back with horror at
the work of the ministry for which he had been supposedly responsible. Charles Townshend was a man of brilliant talents yet
with the overriding shortcomings of extraordinary vanity and

wilfulness, a partiality for drink that earned him the title 'Champagne Charley', and a character blighted through epileptic tendencies. Boastfully he plunged into American affairs in the Commons in January 1767 pledging, without the authority of the Cabinet, the raising of new revenue in the colonies. By May he had won approval for his schemes though not without opposition; yet, as Grafton noted:

No one of the ministry had sufficient authority to advise the dismission of Mr Charles Townshend, and nothing less could have stopped the measures, Lord Chatham's absence being in this instance, as well as others, much to be lamented.

His behaviour until his death in September 1767 was insulting to members of the Cabinet; irresolute and quixotic, he openly ridiculed his political colleagues and intrigued with their opponents. Only in his American schemes did he show constancy.

The Townshend duties were only part of the means to the end of an overall strengthening of British authority in America. A revenue was provided which could be used to defray the costs of civil government and administration of justice, as well as contributing towards the cost of defence. Duties were levied on glass, paint, paper and tea and the estimated yield was £40,000 per annum. Townshend had been defeated in February in his attempt to maintain the English land tax at four shillings in the pound; he kept office and agreed to reduce the tax to three shillings, an annual loss of about £500,000. Thus the American duties were an insignificant contribution to economy. The readiness of the Cabinet to accept the scheme was enhanced by reports of American troubles – of the pardoning of rioters and the refusal to implement the Mutiny Act in New York. Even Chatham was losing patience; only the merchants believed the move inappropriate and ill-timed.

In June 1767 Townshend gave additional force to the duties by creating an American Board of Customs Commissioners. This was to replace the English board created by Charles II; the new headquarters for the colonies was Boston and all officials, including those for Bermuda and the Bahamas, were under its authority.

Already the customs service had been strengthened by the Sugar Act; this new move was designed to cut down delays and costs. Next, in 1768 an Order in Council established four Vice-Admiralty courts to extend the work hitherto centred on Halifax. Boston, Philadelphia and Charleston were added to hear appeals from provincial courts and also to exercise original jurisdiction. These measures emphasized the power of law and made evasion more difficult, although the extent of the coastline and popular sympathy with the smugglers made total enforcement impossible.

Professor Dickerson believes that 'the tactless, arbitrary, and mercenary operation of these laws by a new race of customs officers' led directly to the crisis of 1775. Customs racketeering, whereby ships were seized through technicalities in the law, hit the financially weakest merchants hardest. Yet the victims also included the wealthy John Hancock of Boston, and Henry Laurens of South Carolina. Officers received one-third of the proceeds of ships condemned and sold for customs violations. Such operations surely contributed to the rapid decline in goodwill between Britain and her colonies.

Peace and quiet had not been absolute in America after the repeal of the Stamp Act. In particular the Mutiny Act of 1765 continued to give offence. This called upon colonial governments which had British troops stationed in their barracks to provide without payment fire, candles, vinegar and salt, bedding, some utensils and drink for the men. Opposition was apparent in Georgia and Massachusetts but most particularly in New York, where the Assembly refused to pay for the upkeep of troops and challenged the authority of Parliament. With the support of Chatham and Camden, Townshend introduced a bill in June 1767 to suspend the legislative power of the New York Assembly. The colony was not supported by its fellows and believing it inappropriate to prolong the issue, came to heel. Yet smouldering hostility lingered.

Opposition to Townshend's Revenue Acts and the later Order in Council was not slow to materialize although trade did not decline as had happened in 1764. Tea was actually cheaper when the threepence a pound duty replaced the old total duty of a shilling.

Merchants maintained their smuggling and a few customs officers were tarred and feathered or mobbed by the local populace; a revenue sloop *Liberty* was burned at Newport, Rhode Island. Yet during this period Boston lost its smuggling trade because the customs officers were supported by troops. The considerable gain to the Exchequer was cancelled out by the decline in public confidence; the use of troops to control colonists in peacetime was bitterly resented as tyranny, despite the situation in which the Americans were themselves the perpetrators of violence.

The merchants also returned to a policy of non-importation from Britain in 1768. Slow at first to respond to the lead given by patriot leaders and town councils they were inflamed by Lord Hillsborough's circular (see below pp. 71–2) and the demand that duties be paid in coin, not paper money. New England and New York took the lead but the southerners were most reluctant because the duties did not affect their livelihood. Merchants were anxious not to arouse the feelings of the mob to fever pitch; they had been alarmed by the extravagant displays during the Stamp Act crisis and now hoped to demonstrate without loss of control. It was important that all merchants should be in agreement. Philadelphia did not join until 1769, after her petitions to the merchants in London had been rejected; even then the agreement between the ports was to press for the repeal of the Townshend duties rather than the radical Bostonian demand for a repeal of all mercantile legislation since 1763. Southern colonies agreed to a black list of goods, but generally southern merchants were hostile and agreements were engineered by the planters. By the autumn of 1769 all colonies, bar New Hampshire, had adopted non-importation clauses, but they were variously worded. Generally speaking all forms of luxury goods were taboo; in Virginia the list included slaves, spirits, beef, sugar, pewter, looking glasses, Indian goods of all sorts except spices, linens of more than two shillings a yard, hats, shoes and many others.

William Palfrey wrote:

the agreement has been generally and strictly adhered to as was possible from the nature of so extensive an undertaking notwithstanding all the opposition it met with from a few individuals.

Prices increased dramatically, building ceased, unemployment was common and only the farmers prospered. Those who defied the ban were ostracized by their fellows and in some cases this entailed bankruptcy or the physical break-up of business through mob intervention. In the South agreements were honoured in Maryland and South Carolina, but Virginians were often too lazy. Imports from England fell – from £2,157,218 in 1768 to £1,336,122 in 1769; likewise exports to England dropped from £1,200,000 to £1,060,000. Yet this did not arouse in English merchants the same support for the colonials as did the Stamp Act legislation. Although the volume of trade slumped dramatically Englishmen were cushioned by the favourable conditions operating in Europe. Harvests were excellent and some prices dropped. An expanding wool market in Germany and a fully occupied economy meant that pressure on the ministry to repeal the duties was marginal. When in January 1770, at the instigation of colonial agents, the London merchants did present a petition to the House of Commons, repeal of the duties had been already determined by the Cabinet and the pressure was in no way decisive.

To compensate for the lack of British luxuries the Americans encouraged their own industries, though few had sufficient capital to develop rapidly enough to benefit from the new market, and no one seriously considered that the embargo of luxury goods would last indefinitely. As a substitute for fine cloth the patriotic took to homespun and made do without wigs; the printers used American paper, tea was planted in New England and vineyards in Virginia; industry was given enormous encouragement and factory life became a reality for some and a vision for others. But America was essentially an agricultural country and the movement away from the old pattern was very limited. It was a game of bluff to persuade the government to repeal the Townshend duties.

However, patriotic feeling was stirred, especially by John Dickinson's *Letters of a Pennsylvanian Farmer*, published between December 1767 and February 1768. He denied the legality of all taxation imposed upon the Americans, though accepting the British right to regulate trade and gain an incidental revenue.

If the intention were to raise taxes (as was the case with Townshend's duties) such legislation was contrary to American rights. But he believed that a course of peace and prudence matched with firmness and cooperation was preferable to violence. The letters appeared originally in the *Pennsylvania Chronicle and Universal Advertiser* and were swiftly reprinted in other newspapers. Later as pamphlets they had immense influence until superseded by Tom Paine's *Commonsense* in 1776. British reaction to these movements was immediate because the basis of merchant wealth was threatened again. Americans were regarded as utterly untrustworthy, and property to be 'perpetually at the mercy of every ruffian who bellows the cause of liberty'.

The constitutional response to the Townshend duties emerged in the Circular Letter of the Massachusetts Assembly in February 1768. Considering it came from Boston it was a conciliatory document but adamant on two points. First, that Parliament in levying taxes on the Americans was granting this property without their consent which was contrary to their natural and constitutional rights. Second, that they did not wish to send representatives to the English Parliament because equal representation would be denied them, and 3,000 miles made the prospect unrealistic. In addition, they objected to the provision of salaries for civil officers from revenue returns, and also to the Mutiny Act. Yet they accepted Parliament as the supreme legislative power over the whole empire but believed that even Parliament was bound by the inalienable rights of man. The letter was approved by the Virginians but the Pennsylvanians were suspicious and took no action.

The letter reached London in April where Lord Hillsborough, recently appointed Secretary of State for the Colonies, took control of the matter. He was a man of singularly limited judgment or tact and his reply in a circular letter to the American governors proved both crude and unimaginative.

His Majesty considers this measure to be of a most dangerous and factious tendency, calculated to inflame the minds of his good subjects in the colonies, to promote an unwarrantable combination and to excite and encourage an open opposition to and denial of the authority

of Parliament . . . it is His Majesty's pleasure that you should immediately . . . exert your utmost influence to defeat this flagitious
attempt to disturb the public peace by prevailing upon the Assembly
of your Province to take no notice of it, which will be treating it with
the contempt it deserves.

Should an Assembly insist upon approving the Massachusetts
letter, it was to be dissolved. The effect of Hillsborough's action
was to unite the Americans as the New England letter had never
done. The government had shown itself inflexible and unwilling
to accept advice when given in a spirit of moderation. Consequently Massachusetts refused to repent and even Pennsylvania
approved.

Deterioration in Anglo/American relations was disagreeably
noticeable. In June 1768 Hillsborough ordered General Gage to
station four regiments in Boston consequent upon the rioting of
March and April. The government was pitifully weak; customs
officers had to take refuge in local forts or warships. Royal
governors found themselves without coercive power and magis-
trates could not secure convictions. Neither life nor property was
safe either to officials or American loyalists, so the solution to call
in troops may have been justified in the context. In 1769 two regiments moved to Halifax and the weakness of the army in Boston
then proved most unfortunate. The soldiers failed to maintain
full control over the townsfolk yet their presence provoked resentment, amply demonstrated in hostile newspaper articles and
public tauntings. Patriots declared war, not with firearms but
with weapons of derision or, at worst, cudgels in alleyways on
dark nights. The restraint of the British troops was noteworthy
and despite extreme provocation serious incidents threatened but
did not materialize. The mob gained courage by the pacific way
troops received such treatment, believing that under no circumstances would they open fire. Only one incident was needed to
provoke bloodshed in early 1770; on 5 March the so called Boston
Massacre occurred.

Conflicting views of the event were presented by the patriot
and military witnesses. Captain Preston stated that on the night
of the 5th the mob threatened the sentry at the customs house

where the common revenue was lodged. He sent thirteen men to help the sentry and went himself to disperse the crowd by talking, but the mood was too ugly for reason. The Americans, throwing snowballs or wielding clubs, jostled the troops and in the mêlée which followed gunshots rang out. The crowd retreated, leaving five dead or dying and seven injured. After returning to pick up the casualties, they reassembled to attack the troops who had in the meantime been reinforced. Thomas Hutchinson, the Lieutenant-Governor, persuaded the patriots to give way, but the immediate transfer of the military from the mainland to Castle William, a fort in Boston Harbour, was seen as a British retreat and a popular victory. Preston and eight soldiers were tried by a local jury in a Boston court in October, six months after the incident, by which time passions had cooled. It was unlikely that Preston ordered the men to shoot, if only because he was himself in direct line of fire, but in the confusion words were uncertain and the men could be excused for believing the order had been given. The Boston patriots attempted to show that the occasion was a plot laid by the troops but the jury upheld the defence, led by John Adams, who was no tory. Two men were found guilty of manslaughter, but Preston and the others were acquitted.

Also by October news of the repeal of all the Townshend duties, except tea, had reached the colonies. Townshend himself had died suddenly in September 1767 without witnessing the troubles which his measures provoked; Grafton had carried the government after Chatham's resignation, but in turn he was succeeded by Lord North who announced the abolition of the duties from 1 December 1770. North, who believed the duties to be injurious to British industry and who denounced them as 'preposterous', left the tea tax partly as an expression of parliamentary right and also because it brought in a revenue of £4,000–£12,000 per annum. The measure posed a problem in the colonies; whether to accept the conciliatory gesture and resume normal trading relations with Britain – or to stand firm on constitutional principles and maintain non-importation.

Two main features determined the American attitude. First, mob violence seemed to have got out of hand. The Boston Massacre was the best example of the retreat from authority into anarchy. New York was also troubled by the case of Alexander McDougall who attacked the Assembly for its agreement to supply British troops under the terms of the Mutiny Act. He was imprisoned but became a popular hero. In so doing he focused the attention of the people on a legislature in which they were as underrepresented as in the House of Commons. The aristocratic families, the Delanceys and Livingstons, controlled politics in the interest of their families and other wealthy landowners of the colony. They had no intention of sharing their power with the people. A tight oligarchy was established, though popular favour was sought and gained by the Delanceys by 1770. The Sons of Liberty were anxious to utilize fully the anti-British feeling to stimulate movement towards a people's democracy, and McDougall was a Scottish agitator fully in sympathy with this ideal. During his three months in prison he was the American equivalent of John Wilkes and the number 45 of the *North Briton* became a magical figure. McDougall received a deputation of 45 men on the 45th day of the year, also on another occasion being visited by 45 virgins who sang 45 songs. A tory commentator rather destroyed this romantic vision by declaring the virgins to be 45 years old. Popular passions ran high in the colony and authority was challenged.

Second, the non-importation agreements showed serious deficiencies. New Hampshire and Rhode Island, for example, had taken advantage of the effective ban in Boston and New York to carry on clandestine trade; in the South, Georgia was suspected by South Carolina. The New York merchants were heartened by the act of Parliament which reached them in June authorizing the issue of £120,000 of paper money within the colony. They now sought to break the non-importation agreement. Despite protests from McDougall, Boston and Philadelphia, but backed by the result of a suspect poll in New York city, trade in all articles except tea reopened in July. A roar of disapproval and charges of desertion were levelled at the city by the faithful of New Jersey, Connecticut and upriver Albany.

Without the integration of New York the scheme of non-importation became impossible. Merchants brought pressure to bear on the radicals and trade was resumed – by Philadelphia in September, Boston in October, Virginia in July 1771. Property holders, both landed and those involved in trade, withdrew often with some sense of relief, out of the clutches of the radicals. Lord North had achieved a singular victory over colonial opposition, without troops or bloodshed, by the application of sweet reasonableness. Tea was smuggled in ever increasing quantities but commerce resumed. Despite the irritating behaviour of the radical fringe, amiability and prosperity reasserted itself in America.

PART III
Prelude to War, 1770-5

[11] AN INTERLUDE

The return to 'normalcy' as President Harding might later have expressed it, was swift and unashamed. Although the aristocrats and merchants of New York were henceforth viewed with considerable suspicion by fellow Americans and were roughly handled by some when they ventured out of the colony, the removal of trade barriers was greeted enthusiastically. With the resumption of the old commercial links, fervour for chauvinistic Americanism diminished. The New York decision to break non-importation might have been politically unworthy but soon most people experienced its business wisdom. Many native manufactures were cast aside in favour of traditional imports; in Charleston, South Carolina for example, the shipwrights and coopers were most unhappily placed by 1773. Yet generally the whole tenor of life became more relaxed – the ladies supped tea and the gentlemen gave up the querulous subject of politics. Not only was a more friendly climate of opinion formed but the resumption of old ways led to considerable prosperity. This was a factor which strengthened loyalist feelings and which led the British government into a false position in 1773 when it believed the tea troubles would be shortlived because of the financial stake involved.

So strong were the merchants in 1770 that they were able to import bullion from England and barely to notice the continuation of the old mercantilist regulations. Of the Townshend duties only the tea tax remained. The wholesale evasion of the law by Dutch smugglers with tea at twenty shillings a pound meant that illicit and reasonably priced supplies met the needs of the majority of Americans. Decisions made in 1770 stated that taxed tea should continue to be boycotted, but so indifferent were the colonists that taxed tea was openly brought into ports other than New York or Philadelphia; it is reckoned that in 1771 ninety per cent of the tea was smuggled. Merchant prosperity helped colonial finance, too; Massachusetts freed herself from debt and created a surplus with supplies assured from the growing volume of sales of public lands.

Yet all was not entirely peaceful. Within the colonies themselves troubles flared up. By far the most serious was the Regulator movement in North Carolina where upcountry farmers, who had been originally drawn together to oppose British oppression, soon found objectives nearer home. The planter-dominated Assembly refused to give adequate representation to the growing hinterland population nor would they ensure justice in the western counties. Thus the cry of 'No taxation without representation' was directed locally rather than to London. In December 1770 the assembly passed laws against rioting, but the Regulators refused to comply. The royal governor raised sufficiently large forces to march inland and in 1771 at the battle of the Alamance river the rebels, virtually leaderless, were hopelessly defeated. Dissenters moved further west, while those who accepted the amnesty remained. When the assembly joined the revolutionary movement in 1775 many of the old Regulators became loyalists in order to destroy the tidewater aristocracy.

Boundary disputes also disturbed the internal peace of America. New Englanders and Pennsylvanians fought out their grievances in western Pennsylvania; disputes in New Hampshire when New York land grabbers claimed territory led to the tough activities of the Green Mountain boys who successfully defended the area from the intruder. Disputes also continued between governors and their assemblies; radicals tried to find excuses for maintaining opposition to the British government but until 1772 without conspicuous success.

The earliest sign that this period of peace and prosperity might be illusory was the *Gaspee* incident of March 1772. Commanded by Lieutenant Dudington the *Gaspee*, an armed schooner, appeared off Rhode Island and began to interfere with smuggling. Dudington was so efficient that he was quickly recognized as an enemy of the people. Men burnt with indignation and their fury was expressed when the schooner ran aground off Providence. The opportunity was too good to be missed. Patriot crews rowed out to the ship, boarded her, put bullets into the arm and groin of her commander, set him adrift in an open boat, and then burned her. This deliberate attack on the authority of the Crown demanded investigation, but the Commission of Inquiry failed to acquire a body of evidence which would enable it to act. The Rhode Islanders, who bitterly complained of the inquisitorial nature of the commission, especially its power to hold suspects for trial in England, carefully covered their tracks so that no culprit was found. Authority was dealt a heavy blow by the failure of the government to achieve convictions or to deal out punishment. For his pains and loyalty Dudington was promoted to captain, but government vessels relaxed their grip and in 1773 seizures of illicit cargoes fell by almost 60 per cent.

Authority in New England was dealt another sharp blow by the publication in 1773 of the Hutchinson/Oliver correspondence. Thomas Hutchinson, when Lieutenant-Governor, had written privately to an M.P., Thomas Whately, expressing his views on the American disturbances. The letters did not add significantly to opinions he had already publicly declared. Andrew Oliver, another of the Massachusetts oligarchy, had written likewise to English friends. Benjamin Franklin obtained the letters in London and sent them to New England supposedly for private circulation. Patriot leaders thought fit to publish the letters to discredit the writers; in this they may be considered successful in that Oliver died in 1774, and Hutchinson was replaced as governor by General Gage. The attack on Hutchinson was in many ways unfair; although a tory he wished to maintain the charter of Massachusetts intact, and he believed that mob action could only antagonize the British and destroy the fabric of reasonable government as exercised by Americans like himself. The Coercive Acts confirmed his worst imaginings.

Instrumental in the destruction of calm in Anglo/American relations after the *Gaspee* incident was Sam Adams (1722–1803) in Boston. He had been educated at Harvard and later studied law; he then transferred to the business world but failed to make good. After his father's death in 1748 he gradually frittered away his inheritance and by 1758 was in serious financial trouble. By 1764 Adams, a tax collector, owed Boston about £8,000 in tax arrears. Throughout his life he remained singularly inept in managing his own affairs and relied upon the generosity of friends to provide for the necessities of his family, while he remained unconcerned.

Yet his dabbling in local politics was far more successful, and from 1764 he was a primary source of grievance for both the British administration and American tories such as Hutchinson. Adams used both the Sugar and Stamp Acts to denounce such a man, and he fired the Boston mob to violence, although always careful to screen his own part in proceedings. From 1764 until 1774 he was a member of the Massachusetts House of Representatives which, under his influence as Clerk of the House, became exceedingly radical. A running battle between the Governor and the House ensued.

Adams's interests were linked with the Sons of Liberty and in his writings, which were extraordinarily prolific under a variety of noms de plume, he gradually moved away from the concept of loyalty to Great Britain to consider the natural rights of men and the place of colonial legislatures. In this way he gained a reputation both as a popular leader and polemical writer of distinction. Probably his greatest contribution to the radical cause was during the years 1770–3. In 1770 he was one of the few who maintained an actively patriot viewpoint. Most of his companions since 1765 had bowed out of political life; John Hancock returned to commerce and John Adams had lost face through his defence of Captain Preston at the trial of those concerned with the 'Boston Massacre'. Only Sam remained to vent his grievances in a bitter and unrelenting tone in the press. Under no illusion about the true direction of merchant interests, he was prepared to use the propertied classes as far as possible, and was indeed surprised that they should have been so enthusiastic before 1770. Their retreat into reaction caused him little surprise although he fought hard to keep alive the rebellious instincts of the wealthy Hancock.

An even greater contribution than newspaper articles was made by Adams between 1770 and 1773. This was the institution of Committees of Correspondence. He persuaded the town meeting in Boston to elect a committee to communicate with similar towns about their rights and feelings related to the current political situation. The *Gaspee* affair helped, as did the creation in 1772 of a civil list to pay the salaries of the royal governor and judges in Massachusetts from the customs revenue, a move interpreted as an attempt to make the officials independent of popular control. In November 1772 Adams drafted a letter containing a most persuasive list of grievances which was accepted for circulation throughout Massachusetts. Radicals quickly responded and in his history Thomas Hutchinson noted:

From a state of peace, order and general contentment the province was brought into a state of contention, disorder and general dissatisfaction.

As governor he denounced the movement which in March 1773 was taken up by the Virginians. Its impetus continued into the spring of 1774 when the organization was seen to be popularly based and not dependent upon the support of the merchants. Yet the movement was strengthened by a common cause between both patriot and merchant over Lord North's Tea Act.

[12] THE BOSTON TEA PARTY

Lord North had kept the tax on tea in 1770 as a symbol of the power of the British government to determine taxation; it was the outward and visible sign of the meaning of the Declaratory Act. In 1773, however, it was not the desire to tax the colonies which created the tea dispute, but rather the affairs of the East

India Company. This mammoth concern, chartered in 1600, held immense power in India. Inspired by Clive's military victories it had relegated the French to an inferior position by 1757 and had assumed control over large areas of the country, especially Bengal. Company officials abused the powers invested in them and widespread corruption followed, despite Clive's attempt to install responsible government. Parliament recognized the Company's authority in 1767; an annual levy of £400,000 was charged by the Exchequer for the privilege, a sum which Clive believed could be paid out of a trading surplus.

Yet by 1770 the company had been given over £1 million to avoid bankruptcy. Parliamentary enquiries were set on foot with a two-fold result in 1773. First, a Regulating Act was passed by which the Company in return for the liquidation of its debts had to submit to controls laid down by Parliament, measures later radically adjusted by Pitt's India Act of 1784. Secondly, and more important in American affairs, there was the Tea Act, which allowed the passage of tea directly from India to America, thus eliminating the middlemen's profits in England. Stocks of tea amounted to seventeen million pounds weight, so new outlets had to be found if prosperity were to return. American delight in tea drinking was well known – so was the high incidence of Dutch smuggled tea. The argument ran that if the price of smuggled tea were undercut, then not only would the Americans be delighted but also the Company would rapidly regain solvency. Direct trading enabled Company tea to sell at ten shillings a pound – a half that of the smugglers.

Two features of this move were likely to cause dismay among the colonists, despite their delight at the prospect of a cheaper drink. The first was the retention of the tea tax of threepence a pound. Directors of the Company had tried to persuade Lord North to remove this, but he remained firm believing not only in the principle of parliamentary taxation, but also that, if the overall price of tea were sufficiently low, Americans would not object to the tax. Secondly, the colonists saw the threat of monopoly. The company sent the tea to a group of selected merchants who were to distribute it to dealers; once the trade was established then what would prevent company agents excluding the merchants? By a flight of American imagination the Company was seen to embark on a policy to destroy all local trade and to reduce the colonists to a status as subservient as that of the Indians. This fear was heightened by the fact that the Company dealt not only in tea but in silks, calicoes, spices and chinaware and might put pressure on the government to allow direct trade with America in these articles also. John Dickinson summed up:

The Monopoly on Tea, is, I dare say, but a small Part of the Plan they have formed to strip us of our Property. But thank God, we are not Sea Poys, nor Mahrattas, but BRITISH SUBJECTS who are born to Liberty, who know its worth, and who prize it high.

Sam Adams and the Committees of Correspondence demanded a boycott of tea. In their fervour the patriots invented weird reasons for abstinence:

Do not suffer yourself to sip the accursed, dutied STUFF, for if you do, the devil will immediately enter into you, and you will instantly become a traitor to your country.

Dr Young, a Bostonian much concerned with the body political too, quoted a European opinion that tea was responsible for prevalent diseases such as 'spasms, vapours, hypochondrias, palsies, dropsies, rheumatism and consumption'.

Of all tea drinkers women were the most addicted and the success of popular agitation depended on their assent. Whereas Englishmen thought they had found a trump card in female weakness, the ladies wholeheartedly supported the boycott.

Of immense importance in creating opposition to the Tea Act were the merchants. Fear of monopoly and the destruction of their livelihood threw them again, as had the Stamp Act and Townshend duties, into positions of leadership against the Crown. The first outcry came from those engaged in smuggling. They had everything to lose. So the hotbeds of smuggling, New York and Philadelphia, led the way. But the whole body of merchants was concerned with the effect of monopoly and even if there had been no duty on tea, the storm would have been equally great, as newspaper articles of the time show quite clearly. The

cry of taxation was only a whimper compared with the throaty
yelps occasioned by the threat of monopoly, although merchants
realized that popular support for their stand could be better
stimulated by appeals to 'natural rights' and 'liberty' than to
'profit and loss'.

Those merchants honoured by the East India Company with
the privilege of being their 'consignees' for the tea soon realized
their mistake, one similar to that of the stamp masters in 1765.
Pressure was brought to bear and generally they resigned. The
situation in Boston was different. First, the Customs Board was
situated there and troops were available in Castle William, so the
dignity and presence of Crown representatives were felt. Second,
Governor Hutchinson was involved in the dispute. He felt that
weakness would not assist the government's cause; also, since the
publication of his letters, he felt his reputation to be at stake. His
sons were among the consignees and he overestimated the loyalist
element in the town and so was encouraged to take a bold stand.
Third, Sam Adams and the patriots resolved not to be defeated
by either Governor or Company, and were prepared to be as
obstinate as both. Adams realized that this was the opportunity
for action he had awaited for three years; he had drawn Hancock
back into the radical cause and through the Committees of Correspondence he could call on the assistance of radical groups in
neighbouring towns if the merchants proved too conservative.
It was this situation of deadlock which produced the Boston Tea
Party on the night of 16 December 1773.

The tea ship *Dartmouth* arrived on 27 November, followed by
two others some days later. The town meeting was replaced by
the radicals' joint committee which voted that the tea be returned and no duty paid. Only if Hutchinson allowed the ship to
depart would violence be averted because after twenty days the
cargo was likely to be seized by customs for non-payment of duty.
This would involve landing the tea, which the patriots were determined to prevent, fearing that once on land the tea would be
secretly distributed from the customs warehouses by the consignees.

The master of the *Dartmouth* asked leave to depart, but Hut-

chinson refused. Just prior to the twentieth day, therefore, the
radicals took law into their own hands. Three disciplined detachments each of fifty men disguised as Mohawk Indians boarded
the three ships, and with the help of the sailors they lifted about
three hundred chests from the holds, broke them open and heaved
them overboard. Although their Indian disguise was far from
effective the crowds on the quayside prevented any royal officials
gaining close scrutiny. No damage was done to property other
than the tea, all of which was dumped, not carried off; nobody
was injured. The identity of the raiders has never been established
and it is not certain that either Hancock or Sam Adams was
involved. Yet merchant opinion favoured the destruction of
£18,000 worth of East Indian Company goods, an indication of
how far the radicals had gained control.

Similar episodes, to the strains of 'Tea Deum', were enacted
throughout the colonies. The loyalty of New York was affirmed
when the Sons of Liberty put a consignment of tea into the harbour with a band on the quay striking up 'God Save The King'.
In New Jersey and Maryland tea was burnt, in Charleston it was
dumped in the river. Patriots banned the use of tea throughout
the colonies to ensure that no dutied tea whatsoever should be
consumed, even though this was a severe financial blow to the
smugglers.

Violence to tea shipments was not universal and many loads
were returned to the Company without landing. Destruction was
often regarded as unnecessary; many Americans were not prepared to destroy the basic structure of their society in its relationship with the rule of law and the British government. There
was no move for independence here, no desire for anarchy. Each
incident, however, brought nearer the possibility of conflict;
each contributed to the breakdown of understanding between
Lord North and the colonists.

[13] THE COERCIVE ACTS

To some extent the Tea Party clarified the political attitudes of both whig and tory in England and America. Lord North from 1770 had cleverly lain low where American affairs were concerned. He had no dispute with the Americans, and in so far as he possessed good sense and an easy temper he was unlikely to be forced into dogmatic or doctrinal positions which would cause antagonism. Also he was a 'king's man', and the American patriots were more kindly disposed towards the king than towards Parliament. His ministry was also likely to appeal more to Americans; Grafton returned as Lord Privy Seal and, of even greater importance, the evangelical Lord Dartmouth became Secretary of State for the Colonies in place of the savage Hillsborough in 1772. Dartmouth had been a member of the Rockingham administration and favoured conciliation. His personal characteristics of piety and integrity indicated to the colonials that the mother country was not yet totally devoid of political morality, and his intimacy with Lord North that these moderate views were probably shared.

North was an adept sleeper on the Front Bench; he was so successful in removing the colonies from popular gaze that for two years they were not mentioned in parliamentary debates. When stirred into action it was India, not America, that needed attention; in 1773 he entertained no malice towards the colonials, there was no secret assault planned to destroy liberty of person or trade as suggested by patriots. He kept the tea duty as a reasonable tax and expected to be thanked for reducing the cost of the popular drink. When the Boston Tea Party was reported, the issue was seen as one of rank defiance which required the enforcement of authority. Already fed up with colonial nigglings, such as the *Gaspee* incident and in London the duplicity of Benjamin Franklin for his part in the Hutchinson/Oliver correspondence scandal, the government tended to oversimplify the issue; either British supremacy existed in America, or it did not. In deciding to enforce the former, the ministry acted with determination and singular purpose.

It seemed as if the extremist views which had opposed the repeal of the Stamp Act and the Townshend duties were vindicated. Many felt that moderation and decency were now signs only of weakness and cowardice, and that the way to deal with such ingratiates was by force. North did not commit himself to the wholesale physical destruction of Boston but by his Port Act of March 1774, which closed the port to all trade from 1 June, he was prepared to ruin the city economically until repayment was made to the East India Company and officials for their loss. Two great merits seemed attached to this form of action: other northern ports would be delighted if Boston were humbled and removed from competition; also the minimal cost and relative efficiency of blockading the port appealed to orderly minds.

A second 'Coercive Act' followed in May – the Massachusetts Government Act. Whereas by long tradition the council had been elective and therefore comparatively free of royal control, now it became appointive; the governor was given full power over local law officers; town meetings were restricted and the appointment of juries altered. General Gage, who was on holiday in England, returned to America both as commander-in-chief of the forces, and Governor of Massachusetts. Authority was given him to bring as many troops as necessary into the colony to maintain order.

At the same time the Administration of Justice Act was passed – called by Americans, 'The Murder Act'. Any official, either civil or military, accused of a capital offence in Massachusetts could be tried in Britain or another colony; this protected over-zealous officials who committed murder in the course of their duties and would not gain a fair trial from local juries. In June the Quartering Act allowed the billeting of troops away from barracks in uninhabited houses, barns or other buildings, thus giving the military forces far wider scope in their movements. Whereas the first three acts applied only to Massachusetts, this last act operated in every colony. All these bills passed easily through Parliament. Only Burke and a handful of followers championed moderation and expressed fearful expectations for the future.

In the opinion of most colonists a fifth coercive act was passed in June 1774 – the Quebec Act. Since 1763 the province had been unsettled and the 'anglicanization' so eagerly hoped for failed to materialize, with the result that French Roman Catholic interests remained predominant. Every ministry was faced with this problem and in 1771 law officers began to prepare a settlement. By 1773 North had ample information to draft an act and was receptive to arguments for immediate action before the Tea Party created the new crisis. The problem involved not only Quebec and the St Lawrence river area, but also the territory beyond the Proclamation line of 1763 up to the Mississippi. The need to protect the Indians and to prevent land grabbing by individual speculators created dangerous pressures which could not be borne indefinitely. Lord Dartmouth advocated the restoration of the old boundaries of Quebec prior to 1763, which would extend the province behind the thirteen colonies south to the Ohio river.

Although the problems were longstanding and the solutions arrived at without reference to affairs in the other colonies in 1773, the timing of the act was more than coincidental. The government wanted to prevent Canada making common cause with the malcontents; that would have shaken the empire to its roots. Yet the measures were designed to encourage Canadians rather than oppress the others.

There were four main provisions:

1. the governor and his bi-racial (British/French) council kept legislative power (thus maintaining unrepresentative power, because there was no popular assembly)
2. old French laws relating to property and civil rights were to be maintained; English criminal law was to be enforced
3. Roman Catholics were given religious freedom
4. the boundaries were extended westward up the St Lawrence and, more important, south to the Ohio river and west to the Mississippi (see map on page 21)

Objections were particularly obvious to the last two clauses. It appeared that the British government was a convert to Rome and was encouraging Catholicism in the New World in a deliberate

attempt to undermine democracy. New England patriots, strong
in their Protestantism, predicted the worst:

we may live to see our churches converted into mass houses, and
lands plundered of tithes for the support of a Popish clergy.

The inquisition may erect her standard in Pennsylvania and the city
of Philadelphia may yet experience the carnage of a St Bartholomew's
Day

shrieked the *Pennsylvania Packet and General Advertiser*,
further south. Satirical drawings and literature circulated freely
depicting Lord North and the Pope as intimate friends plotting
to turn over the empire to Rome.

A second objection was the extension of Quebec's boundaries.
Land speculators, including George Washington and Patrick
Henry, suddenly found their investments ruined. The area north
of the Ohio seemed dead for the advance of white settlement;
whereas the 1763 line had an element of temporary expediency
about it, the new act implied that the western lands generally
were to be denied to Protestants and given over to Indians and
Catholics.

It was hardly to be expected that the English colonists would
view the Quebec Act with equanimity. It seemed to provide the
government with an army against Protestant subjects; in its
tolerance and justice to Canadians it was encouraging political
and religious beliefs which were anathema. Its effect was two-
fold – Canadians were drawn to the British side when war broke
out, but prior to that, it gave an impetus to the radical cause in
the colonies in a way that only the Stamp Act had succeeded in
doing previously. Although Bostonians may have gone too far in
destroying the property of the East India Company they were
regarded as indeed virtuous by comparison with a government
which could be so devilish.

Why was there so little opposition in Parliament to these
measures? Although political labels in this period were ill-defined
and tempered with countless exceptions the opposition 'whigs'
were scarcely in evidence between 1770 and 1774. Edmund Burke
attacked North and the new toryism in his pamphlet *Thoughts on*

the Causes of the Present Discontents in 1770 hoping to create a new basis for opposition. He claimed that Parliament was a mere appendage of the monarchy and that aristocratic influence was on the wane. By contrast he outlined a whig party under aristocratic leadership and supported by the existing narrowly based franchise. Instead of uniting whigs he emphasized the differences between himself, Chatham (who loathed the notion of party) and the radicals, men who enlisted under the banner of John Wilkes, who loathed aristocrats and the restricted franchise. An opportunity to attack North came with the Boston Tea Party but even then the whigs were hardly effective; they agreed that parliamentary supremacy ought to be maintained and its authority expressed. They could not run the risk of being merely factious; nor did they like the attack on property. The most that they were prepared to do was to try to ensure a fair deal for Boston. Although the debate was long, the Port Act passed the Commons without a division. A more forceful attack was launched against the other Coercive Acts. In particular the Quebec Act was denounced, and encouragement was given to the colonists by Burke and Fox to resist the tyrannical law.

The truth was that by 1775 whig opposition was broken on the wheel of distrust. Gouty whig lords and gentry were unwilling to follow either Chatham or Burke, whose approach to American affairs differed drastically in detail if not in spirit. Chatham staunchly maintained the Navigation Acts; he suspected that Burke was prepared to tamper with them if the Americans so wished. Yet whigs distrusted Chatham for his opposition to the Declaratory Act, nor were they sure how far American liberties ought to be conceded. There was no material here for a fight against the ministry. Individual genius could only cast a single vote, and genius then, as now, was distrusted in British political life.

Loyalist feelings towards George III in America were not confined to merchants or aristocrats; they were found through the whole social structure and included bookbinders, barristers and farmers. One area of strength lay in the West, where soldiers and government action could protect settlers from richer neighbours.

Another was the eastern seaboard where tory power was threatened by the growth of democracy, an area which valued its ties with London more deeply than those with the communities of the interior. Especially in New York and Pennsylvania the staunchest tories were the non-English. Cultural and religious minorities were often tory – French-speaking Calvinists, Negroes and Quakers; but Jews and Roman Catholics were generally patriots. Minorities distrusted the power of individuals who could group together to swamp their ideas; the British government seemed to offer firmer guarantees in this respect than the more aggressive new Americanism.

After 1770 the loyalists emerged full of confidence that a quiescent policy would prevent further patriot activity. They failed to take seriously the possibility of revolution and were afraid to cultivate public opinion lest they should raise seven devils worse than the first. No acceptable alternative to Adams's radical propaganda was put forward and the tories failed by default as much as anything. They wanted to return to the peaceful conditions which were reputed to have existed prior to 1763. Anglican clergy and local oligarchs led tory opinion; men like Joseph Galloway in Pennsylvania, and Thomas Hutchinson in Massachusetts, whose career illustrates the weakness of the movement. As Governor from 1771 he was delighted by Sam Adams's failure to make the House of Representatives a radical machine; prosperity was in full spate. Most radicals were of obscure origins – old Governor Shirley remarked petulantly, 'Mr Cushing I knew, and Mr Hancock I knew, but where the devil this brace of Adamses came from, I knew not'; complacency ruled tory ways; no attempt was made to cross colonial boundaries and create a party or a common policy – Hutchinson did not even know the names of fellow tories in New York or Pennsylvania. Local problems occupied attention and organization was regarded as unnecessary. Eyes turned east towards London rather than north and south to each other.

The harsh legislation in the Coercive Acts seriously undermined the tory position. Hutchinson was relieved by General Gage and reliance on the British government was now seen to be dishonourable. Loyalty to the king remained, despite George's recognition of Parliamentary supremacy. Until Tom Paine's *Commonsense* debunked the king and showed him to be as great a scourge as Parliament, the tories could count on a measure of support from the moderates. Faced with a hostile Parliament, an unsympathetic king and American radical organization, the tory was at the mercy of events. Like Lord North he could only hope that American self-interest would reassert itself and Boston would be deserted by her neighbours.

[14] THE FIRST CONTINENTAL CONGRESS

Boston heard of the Port Act on 14 May. Contrary to Lord North's expectation defeatism was not the immediate reaction. Although some merchants saw the possibility of ruin if British rule were again defied, other Americans, such as Benjamin Franklin, who had condemned the Tea Party, were won over to the radical cause by the Coercive Acts. Nor was the city left isolated. The argument that if Boston were allowed to fall then the privileges of the colonies would be subsequently attacked in turn by the government was generally accepted; the image of Boston had never shone so bright and the eastern seaboard rallied to her aid. Anglicans in Virginia praised her moral and political virtues, and her martyrdom united rather than divided. From 1 June the port was closed and the people were supposed to begin suffering; but through the practical aid of gifts of sheep, wheat, rice and fish even the poorest townsfolk survived remarkably well.

For Sam Adams, to survive was not enough. The Committees of Correspondence in Massachusetts immediately called for a Solemn League and Covenant to cease trading with Great Britain until the Port Act was repealed. Merchants were thoroughly alarmed at this demand for the renewal of a trade embargo. Everywhere they used their influence to prevent the acceptance of such a drastic measure. Merely to be obstructive was insufficient, so the New York Committee of Fifty-One (a merchant-dominated assembly which had replaced the Committee of Correspondence) proposed a Continental Congress, an appeal already made by Virginian burgesses, and others in Philadelphia and Rhode Island. Merchants feared the outcome of a congress but it seemed the only tactic which would thwart the Covenanters.

A congress had been often suggested by the radicals before, so they were eager to cooperate and capitalize upon the situation. Their cause was much strengthened when news of the other Coercive Acts was received; these confirmed the government's intention to destroy the independence of Massachusetts, and the Quebec Act threatened the religion and westward expansion of every colony.

The First Continental Congress met in Philadelphia on 5 September 1774 and lasted seven weeks. The city was far from being a radical headquarters and the delegates were, for the most part, conservative. John Adams in his disgust said they were, 'one-third Tory, another Whigs, and the rest mongrels'. Fifty-six men were appointed from twelve colonies, Georgia declining to send delegates because she was threatened with an Indian frontier war and desperately needed British troops. Different colonies had chosen their delegates in different ways – some by general assembly, others by specially called conventions, or by committees. Whatever the means, the quality of the men chosen to debate at this technically illegal congress was remarkable. Wisdom, understanding and firmness were shown by tories, aristocrats, old troublemakers and future Presidents: John Adams, George Washington, Christopher Gadsden, Patrick Henry, John Jay and Joseph Galloway.

Initial toasts were drunk to 'The Union of the Colonies' and 'The Union of Britain and the Colonies on a Constitutional Foundation'. Instructions to the delegates were not of a revolutionary nature; the objective generally was to confer on the present troubles and recommend measures which would restore harmony between Great Britain and the colonies. Although potentially rebellious, the congress was not banned by the British

government. Lord Dartmouth hoped some moderate proposals
would emerge; the rest of the ministry seemed untroubled.

From the outset of the congress a division between the radical
and the conservative elements was apparent. The radicals
achieved two swift victories: first, the meeting-place of the Congress was the Carpenters' Hall (not the State House as suggested
by Galloway): second, Charles Thomson, leader of the radicals
in Pennsylvania, was elected secretary rather than Galloway's
nominee. John Adams played an astute hand. To prevent antag-
onizing the conservative element he spoke and acted with moderation in all things, and allowed the progressive initiative to be taken
by the Virginians. In this way he scotched fears that Massachusetts wanted to use the Congress for its own ends.

Radicalism was soon advanced by two episodes – the Powder
Alarm and the Suffolk Resolves. It was reported that General
Gage had blown up the town of Boston; the emotional tempera-
ture in Philadelphia rose immediately and a call to arms was
readily accepted. Although the news was soon proved false, the
unanimity of the delegates remained a sign of their common
interests.

Shortly afterwards the Resolves from Suffolk County, in
Massachusetts, were accepted. They were sternly anti-British in
repudiating the Coercive Acts and advocating preparations for
the defence of Boston. In this way Congress edged nearer the
possibility of a defensive war, and showed the intention of other
colonies to support New England.

A further success for the anti-British elements was the acceptance of the Continental Association in October. It was agreed
that non-importation and non-consumption of British goods
would operate from 1 December. Some difficulty was experienced
in drawing up a non-exportation statement; the South with its
staple crops would be hit harder than the North, and sectional
differences began to destroy the good temper of the delegates.
Eventually compromise was reached – non-exportation was to be
delayed until September 1775 and rice was to be exempt. Enforcement of these measures was entrusted to committees, composed for the most part of local patriots. They were extremely

zealous in their duties and not only were offenders who drank tea or madeira wine, or who wore English hats, condemned by name in newspapers but in extreme cases they were tarred and feathered or paraded in the streets as ne'er do wells. In creating an effective local organization, the Association was the greatest success of the Congress. Although often unpopular as an extra-legal authority, the Association embodied the transfer of authority from Britain to the colonies. The effectiveness of local committees is seen by the import figures for British goods for 1775 which were 95 per cent down as those for 1774, and the peppering of petitions from the English merchants on to the ministry.

Delegates commonly believed that Britain would not survive a tightly observed Association and that she would swiftly collapse as a commercial power. The fallacy of this view was soon exposed; although America was a rich province for merchant enterprise new markets were increasingly exploited to excellent effect. Some merchants believed that non-importation would break up as it had in 1770; others supported Lord North because it seemed the only way to recover their debts and restore their privileges; a few looked forward to a war and handsome profits. Thus their petitioning in London was that of the minority.

How serious had the tory challenge been during the Congress? After all, they had hoped to forestall non-importation and disloyalty and had obviously failed; they had hoped to mobilize feelings against Bostonians, who had remained so quiet as to present no target. The one piece of tory manoeuvering which came near to success was Joseph Galloway's plan of union. He proposed a Grand Council in America, with members elected by colonial assemblies, to be an American House of Commons, dealing with matters of general importance to more than one colony; all acts had to be acceptable to parliament in London and the Grand Council. The king was to appoint a resident general who would hold veto power over the Grand Council. The scheme was shrewd because it recognized that most Americans wished to maintain close links with Britain and avoid the necessity for war.

To defeat the scheme Sam Adams was prepared to mobilize the Philadelphia mob (as John Pym used the London mob against

Charles I in 1641) but Galloway himself, after the Suffolk Resolves
had been accepted, realized that the radicals were ascendant.
Congress eventually voted to remove all mention of the plan of
union from its minutes; non-conciliation was more atune to the
mood.

Opposition revived against the Association committees. They
were likened to the Spanish Inquisition:

> If I must be enslaved, let it be by a KING at least, and not by a parcel
> of upstart lawless Committee-men. If I must be devoured, let me be
> devoured by the jaws of a lion and not gnawed to death by rats and
> vermin,

so wrote the Reverend Samuel Seabury, an active Anglican
preacher in New York where the tories scored a resounding
success.

In London, Lord North and his ministry could hardly be
satisfied with the outcome of their Coercive Acts. Instead of
taming the Americans, they had inspired resistance on a scale
hitherto unknown. A national assembly of men of rank and wealth
had pinned their colours to the mast of disobedience.

General Gage had replaced Hutchinson as Governor of Massachusetts and had moved the seat of government to Salem, out of
the clutches of the Boston mob. He was overwhelmed by the task
which had been set him. Forced to dissolve the assembly at
Salem, he noted that a loyalist resolution in Boston to pay
compensation to the East India Company was heavily defeated.
No punishment of the tea rioters was forthcoming. The arrival of
the later Coercive Acts in August made his position even more
difficult, and by the autumn of 1774 he admitted that he could
not control the political situation. Calling for more troops, in
the frantic tone of a man who was beginning to lose his nerve, he
believed that New England could be subdued only through
military force.

In London the ministry went off on its summer holiday in mid-
August. Lord North and George III remained firm in their deter-
mination to force the colonies to recognize English sovereignty.
This was not an unthinking attitude, as is often maintained,

but a determination to settle a question which had constantly harassed ministries over the past ten years.

George III wrote to Lord North on 11 September:

The die is now cast, the colonies must either submit or triumph; I do not wish to come to severer measures but we must not retreat; by coolness and an unremitted pursuit of the measures that have been adopted I trust that they will come to submit.

This attitude was commonly shared, although Lord Dartmouth was more hesitant and accommodating.

The government was strengthened by the dissolution of Parliament on 30 September and the subsequent election. Although the life span of the old Parliament would have lasted until the spring of 1775 Lord North had two motives in an early election: to catch the Opposition unawares, and also to deal with American affairs during the winter without the threat of an inevitable dissolution soon after. Lord North had achieved excellent personal relations with many of the borough patrons, and through his masterful inactivity and the low level of the land tax at three shillings had pleased the independents; so there was no chance of his losing control. The new House of Commons, in so far as government supporters numbered 321 out of a House of 558, was a vote of confidence in the ministry. America was an issue in very few constituencies, possibly under a dozen, and only in Bristol did the matter loom large. There the merchants were desperately anxious to avoid war and were highly displeased with their members who had supported the Coercive Acts. Two new members, both whigs, were therefore elected – the American Henry Cruger, and Edmund Burke, the most distinguished orator in the Commons.

News of the Continental Association strengthened the Cabinet's resolution to be firm. Lord Dartmouth alone worked for conciliation, and his one hope of success was that with the obvious failure of the Coercive Acts by January 1775, a new policy might be attempted. Lord North, pacific by temperament, wished to be moderate, and in his Conciliatory Propositions in February he showed that the government hoped to avoid war. In return for the Americans' recognition of British legislative supremacy he suggested that the colonists should tax themselves through their assemblies. At the same time a pardon was offered to all in Massachusetts who had been responsible for treasonable offences, but the confession which had to be signed was so humiliating an affair that no self-respecting American could accept such conditions.

In offering terms Lord North horrified his supporters in the House of Commons. They demanded blunt confrontation. North had reasons for his offer: he wished to pacify moderate opinion in England; he hoped to split the Americans, and to avoid being held responsible if war came.

Yet, if Lord North were prepared to be conciliatory, he was also prepared to continue waving a big stick. Two acts to restrain the trade of New England, later extended to all the colonies except Georgia and New York, were passed early in 1775 and additional troops with three major-generals left England to bolster up Gage's sagging morale. These acts were virtually an ultimatum – see sense or fight. In practice neither the Conciliatory Proposals or Trade Restraint Acts had much effect because fighting had already broken out at Lexington and Concord before the Americans knew of their existence.

Before returning to American reactions, mention must be made of distinguished attempts in Parliament to avoid war. In January 1775 Chatham passionately defended colonial actions:

Let this distinction remain; taxation is theirs, commercial regulation is ours. As an American I would recognize to England her supreme right of regulating commerce and navigation: as an Englishman, I recognize to the Americans their supreme unalienable right in their property; a right which they are justified in the defence of to the last extremity. To maintain this principle is the common cause of the whigs on the other side of the Atlantic and on this. "Tis liberty to liberty engaged', that they will defend themselves, their families, and their country.

He proposed, therefore, the withdrawal of troops from Boston to prevent a clash which might precipitate a crisis. The motion was defeated.

In February he introduced a bill 'for settling the Troubles in America'. This recognized parliamentary control of trade but in other respects met colonial demands wholeheartedly. Internal taxation by Britain was to be abandoned; Congress was to be recognized and encouraged to arrange its own method of raising an American revenue; the Coercive Acts were to be repealed; and colonial charters were to be guaranteed. Chatham saw that the empire for which he, more than any other, had been responsible, was about to disintegrate.

Edmund Burke spoke in March and achieved a personal oratorical triumph. He recognized the need to 'comply with the American spirit'. This too would have entailed the withdrawal of the coercive legislation and acceptance of self-imposed taxation. The general principles of trust and cooperation which he laid down are among the most powerful arguments for British Constitutional rule. He warned the Commons:

Do not dream that your instructions and your suspending clauses are the things which hold together the great contexture of this mysterious [Empire] . . . it is the spirit of the English communion that gives all their life and efficacy to them. It is the spirit of the English constitution which, infused through the mighty mass, pervades, feeds, unites, invigorates, vivifies every part of the empire, even down to the minutest member.

Although members congratulated Burke both on the matter and manner of his speech, they rejected totally his scheme for free association and trust. Certainly for some radicals in America no gesture by Britain would be satisfactory, so rapidly were the diehards gaining control. It is equally true that by April 1775 no such gesture would be made by Lord North.

[15] LEXINGTON AND CONCORD

General Gage found Massachusetts impossible to control. From his arrival in May 1774 until his recall in August 1775, he was a most unhappy man. Before he arrived in Boston he had believed that the colonists could be worsted without trouble, but gradually the situation deteriorated and with the failure of the Coercive Acts he wrote in September 1774 that, 'civil government is near its end.' Opposed not just by a rabble but by men of rank, he saw a solution only in an outright military coup. The possibility was denied him because he had an insufficient force and no preparations on a war footing. He gained some reinforcements from Canada as well as ships and men from Britain, but his total strength was nowhere near the 20,000 he required. Confidence in Gage waned at home, but it was not until April 1775 that Generals Howe, Clinton and Burgoyne sailed to cheer him up. His position was unenviable; he had to implement thoroughly unpleasant legislation in a bitterly hostile land. Non-cooperation was rife and, despite the willingness of innkeepers to make a profit from his men, the town of Boston refused to provide barracks and carpenters refused to build them, and winter supplies were denied the troops camping on the Common.

Gage was no fire-eater; he was unrefined, anxious to be fair and patient. He failed to please the tories of Boston who wanted a showdown, yet he was reduced to blustering and issuing threats which were likely to drive him into war. The troops were hated by the populace who, as in the days before the Boston Massacre, accused them of all kinds of crime against humanity, women in particular. The Daughters of Liberty were now as important as the Sons! Throughout the winter patriots were preparing for war. Companies of volunteers were formed, stores collected and information passed. Gage knew of their activity and was anxious not to give occasion for bloodshed. If he were to venture beyond Boston the first shots might be fired, because fervour outside the city was at a higher pitch than within. Englishmen generally despised these military preparations – the local militia was indeed raw and ungainly – but most of the men possessed courage and could shoot with accuracy.

On the night of 18 April 1775 Gage sent 800 troops to seize powder at Concord, eighteen miles away, and if possible to arrest John Hancock and John Adams who were reported to be in hiding near Lexington, a village en route. Instead of dead secrecy being maintained, the patriots were warned of the British approach by Paul Revere, who galloped out of Boston on his historic mission. Consequently when the troops arrived at Lexington they found the local patriots drawn up in line on the Common. Who made the first hostile move? The British and American accounts disagree and the evidence is confused. The fact is that shots rang out and men lay dead.

The troops pushed on to Concord where they destroyed only part of the powder store before they were fired on by patriots; they did not find Hancock or Adams. Their return to Boston was difficult and can only be accounted a patriot victory. As a result of accurate sniping 244 casualties were incurred by the British. 'The shot heard round the world' is a traditional description of the Concord episode. Certainly the reaction of the colonists was immediate; unity was established; the commercial associations became defence associations, weapons were purchased and ammunition collected; men were enlisted and money was raised; loyalists were branded as 'enemies of American liberty' and were ostracized or even fined and imprisoned; freedom of speech disappeared. Concord made the situation clearer and made many feel that war could no longer be avoided.

Confirmation of the drift of events was seen in May when colonists captured the royal forts at Ticonderoga and Crown Point, south of Lake Champlain on the direct route from Canada to the Hudson river. This prevented a quick British thrust down the Hudson to New York; it also gained a position of vantage for the Americans from which to invade Canada. In June the battle of Breed's (or Bunker) Hill was fought outside Boston. Local patriots occupied the hill overlooking both harbour and city, a position commanding and defensible. To prevent a permanent encampment and to destroy any fortifications, the British launched

a frontal attack confident that they would meet no serious opposition. In gaining their objective they received over 1,000
casualties, 40 per cent of their force, a loss which undermined the
fighting capacity of the regiments as well as their morale. By
midsummer American militancy had been well rewarded.

[16] THE SECOND CONTINENTAL CONGRESS

Three weeks after Lexington, on 10 May 1775, the Second Continental Congress met at Philadelphia. This body remained in
existence until 1789 when elections under the new constitution
were held for the first time. Members were again chosen in a
haphazard way but now the problems were more intricate and
weighty. Concord was commonly accepted as a declaration of war
in fact if not in intent, and there was the need to determine the
organization of armies and the establishment of central authority,
as well as attending to matters arising from the working of the
Continental Association.

Membership of the Congress was stronger than before. Georgia,
unrepresented earlier, now sent a delegation; among new delegates were Benjamin Franklin and Thomas Jefferson. Among
members returned for a second term were George Washington
and John Adams. These four men were among the most influential of their time and brief biographies here might be helpful in
placing later actions in perspective.

Benjamin Franklin (1706–90) has already featured in the
events so far recorded. Born the tenth son of a soapmaker, he
left school at ten to become an apprentice printer. By the age of
seventeen he was truly expert and had also begun a course of
reading and writing which led to the development of his considerable natural talents: arithmetic, philosophy, literature – all
were part of his interests. He had become sole owner of a flourishing printing works in Philadelphia by the time he was twenty-

four and took an active part in expanding the business until 1748 when he retired on an annual salary of £1,000 plus an income from property and a governmental deputy-postmastership – a man of obvious means and independence.

Throughout his life he had the knack of self-advertisement; his *Poor Richard's Almanack* (1732–57), a series of adventures among ordinary people, brought fame and prosperity; his adoption of simple clothes, even in Paris in 1776, drew favourable comment. His books, benign and yet shrewd, invited trust. With his homely and unintelligent wife, his two legitimate and one illegitimate children, here was a man of the people.

On what does his fame lie? First, on his intellectual achievements. From 1737 onward he wrote scientific papers; his work on electricity and his observation of the natural world was extraordinary. His capacity for argument, political, literary and scientific, was immense and rational, and his writings often affected government decisions. Second, he is well known for his work in England from 1757 until 1775 as a political agent, at first for Pennsylvania but later for Georgia, New York and Massachusetts as well. Throughout this troubled period he attempted to represent American interests to Parliament and the people. During the Seven Years' War he argued for the retention of Canada rather than Guadeloupe; he was called before the House of Commons to be questioned on the Stamp Act in 1766 – and his answers were so telling that he contributed greatly to repeal. As time wore on he became less sure of parliamentary sovereignty, although he always favoured conciliation; his dispatch of the Hutchinson/ Oliver letters to New England in 1773 favoured the patriot cause, although their eventual publication was not his doing, and he was roundly condemned in London as a 'thief and incendiary'. Only in 1775 did he become a radical.

Third, Franklin is revered for his influence on American affairs. The day after his return from England he was chosen as a delegate to the Second Continental Congress, and as such was no stranger to the political world since he had sat in the Pennsylvania Assembly for Philadelphia 1751–64. At the Congress he sketched out a plan of union (he had already drafted one plan, in 1754 at

Albany, to unite the colonists against the French and Indians)
and was appointed to the committee drafting the Declaration of
Independence. At the very end of his life he was President of the
Executive Council of Pennsylvania and a member of the Constitutional Covention of 1787. In these and countless other tasks
Franklin's influence was immense, especially through his qualities of tolerance and humour (though his ideas were not often
adopted).

Finally, there is his work during the years in France, 1776-83.
Already well known through the character of Poor Richard, his
scientific work and previous visits, he was given an immensely
enthusiastic reception by the French for whom he embodied a
real part of the Age of Enlightenment. Naturally their anti-
British sentiment boosted his welcome! He promoted the American cause with fervour and skill. As will later become apparent,
French assistance to the revolutionary struggle was crucial and
the extent of it owed much to the impact of Franklin, whom
Jefferson called, 'The greatest man and ornament of the age and
country in which he lived'.

Thomas Jefferson (1743–1826) was fortunate in his birth since
his mother was a member of the Randolph family, true Virginian
aristocrats. He inherited 2,750 acres of land and later owned
10,000 acres, although a burden of debt never left him and certainly clouded his last years. At an early age he received a classical education, which he always treasured and expanded, and instruction in mathematics and science, all of which appealed to
his basically serious nature. Like the Adamses he trained and
practised as a lawyer until the Revolution. Particularly noteworthy was the range and depth of his interests. Insatiable
curiosity involved him in philosophy, natural science, farming,
medicine, geology, astronomy and meteorology. Essentially he
was a thinker with a practical bent, and this utilitarian attitude
spilled over into his consideration for the arts. Literature he regarded as valuable for the improvement which it offered, and he
tried to establish public libraries in the young republic. Fundamental to his lifework was an unshaken faith in the American
people, in their commonsense and ultimate triumph. This belief in a

progressive society became a vital part of the American political tradition.

In 1769 Jefferson entered the Virginian House of Burgesses. He was a friend of Patrick Henry and sympathized with the protests of the upper county farmers although he was never an effective orator, here or elsewhere. It was in committee that he was immensely strong; not only was he anti-British but he had the ability to state a case on paper. For one so young (he was only thirty in 1773) he had a swift path to fame, especially when his pamphlet *A Summary View of the Rights of British America* appeared in 1774; in this he saw that American allegiance was owed only to the Crown to whom there was a voluntary submission. This denial of parliamentary authority, coupled with a belief that colonial union was only for the advantage of Britain, and claims for free trade with the withdrawal of parliamentary taxation, was too near a position of independence for most Americans in 1774.

Jefferson came to the Second Congress with Peyton Randolph. His part was marginal until, in June 1776, he served on the committee to draft a Declaration of Independence. He was thirty-three at the time, and it was his pen, rather than that of Franklin, which was primarily responsible for the form of that document. Later in 1776 he withdrew from Congress to sit in the House of Delegates in Virginia, where he worked for the divorce of church and state (he had earlier lost faith in conventional religious belief), religious freedom, and the abolition of entail and primogeniture, forms of landholding which he believed to be reactionary. He became Governor of Virginia in 1779, but his two years in office were stormy and his reputation was not enhanced. More important for the American cause was his position as ambassador in Paris between 1784 and 1789, where he built on the foundations laid by Franklin for understanding between France and the New World. His later career as a minister under Washington, his clash with Alexander Hamilton and eight years as the third President of the United States confirmed the early promise of an original and powerful mind.

Despite these achievements Jefferson's personal life remains

A.W.I.—4*

curiously in the shadows. His writings and opinions were of a public rather than private character. For ten years he was happily married, but his wife died in 1782. They had six children, but their only son died in infancy. He never remarried and probably the loss of his wife drove him to a more active public life than would otherwise have been the case. On his tombstone he asked for these words to be written, 'the author of the Declaration of Independence, the Statute of Virginia for religious freedom, and father of the University of Virginia.'

George Washington (1732–99) was born in Virginia and, despite his father's death in 1743, the family was adequately provided for and, as a result of a prudent marriage by his half-brother into the Fairfax family, George was not without influence. He became a surveyor and worked in the Shenandoah Valley, by 1750 laying claim to 1,450 acres on his own behalf. On the death of his half-brother he became wealthy and by the age of twenty-one he was landowner, freemason, major in the Virginian militia, independent and obviously ambitious. This led him to seek military glory and between 1753 and 1758 he was involved in the war with the French along the western boundaries. Some of his exploits showed immense courage in difficult surroundings; in 1754 he led an expedition into the area of the Ohio, and the first shots in a war which was to involve the whole of Europe, were fired by Major Washington's men; in 1755 he was a volunteer member of General Braddock's ill-fated army which was destroyed by the French. When large-scale campaigns began in 1756 the focus of attention moved north to Canada, and Washington felt a sense of anti-climax and frustration. Although he was an honorary brigadier by the time he left military duties in 1758, he had failed either to ensure the security of the Virginian frontier or to obtain the regular army commission which he had sought most eagerly.

So he retired (aged twenty-six), married a wealthy widow and settled down as a landowner at Mount Vernon. He was a burgess at the colonial assembly, a county magistrate and churchwarden as well as a land speculator, expecting the interior, beyond the Appalachians, to open up and yield a rich harvest. Although he ran his estates carefully he was in debt to British merchants, and tried to diversify his crops to compensate for the low price of tobacco. His loyalty to Britain was deep but the Townshend duties stirred him sufficiently to take a leading role in the Virginian non-importation agreements of 1769–70. His passions cooled between 1770 and 1773 but the Coercive Acts dismayed him, although he was far from an extremist of the nature of Patrick Henry. Like many others he was prepared to move towards open defiance of an unreasonable British administration; as a Virginian he felt impelled to protect his property, prospects and way of life. Although by no means an orator of distinction, his views were so respected and his status such that he was elected one of the seven Virginian delegates to the First Continental Congress. There he showed himself reserved, yet sensible and sincere – the type of man about whom both radicals and conservatives could feel confident.

The Second Congress moved to appoint a general for the defence of American liberties. John and Sam Adams proposed Washington and the nomination was carried unanimously. Although only forty-three and not necessarily the most accomplished soldier in the colonies, he was experienced, rich, a Virginian and undoubtedly patriotic. Military preferment which had previously eluded him was now gloriously achieved. The choice of Congress was eminently sound; during the coming years Washington displayed the ability to fight on when disaster struck, as it did during the New York campaign of 1776; to keep an army in the field despite lack of support from Congress; and he showed personal characteristics which all men could admire and which made him in 1789 the first President of the United States. For eight years he served with great integrity, believing in strong government and the need to create financial stability. No nation could have been more fortunate in its choice of president.

Although sometimes difficult to separate the man from the legend, Washington's is a character to honour. Not an intellectual like Jefferson or Franklin, his presence was often reserved and unentertaining. His ambition developed from being largely personal to include a new nation. By religion he was an Episcopalian,

but without fuss, probably lacking conviction. He was generous
with money and indefatigable in public office. The greatness of
the man lies in the sum total of his achievements more than in
individual details; he was soldier, administrator, and figurehead.
In each he showed less than genius, but in combining all three so
skilfully he gave distinction to his nation.

John Adams (1735–1826), who became second President of the
United States in 1797, studied law at Harvard and was called to
the bar in Boston in 1758. Prospering slowly, he took part in
town politics and through his marriage in 1764 gained worthwhile introductions to well-placed Massachusetts families. He
first came into prominence with his opposition to the Stamp Act
and a number of legal actions, especially his defence of John
Hancock on a smuggling charge, identified him with the patriot
cause. Bravely he undertook the defence of Captain Preston for
his part in the Boston Massacre in 1770, because Adams believed
in his innocence and was opposed to mob violence. This did not
endear him to the radical leaders, and like many other prominent
citizens he withdrew from politics between 1770 and 1773 until
stirred by the Tea and Coercive Acts. When chosen as a delegate
to the First Continental Congress his attitude had not been dog-
matically formulated, but his shrewdly exercised powers in
debate, especially the ability to know when to keep silent or
appear meek, much enhanced the radical cause. His exasperation
was often found in his private correspondence but his public
image was of oriental inscrutability.

Because of events at Lexington, Congress was in a fighting
mood in the spring of 1775. The need to defend their land was
recognized by the delegates and an army of 20,000 was demanded. John Adams, anxious to draw the South closer to New England in military matters, suggested Washington as commander-in
chief, a choice which appealed greatly. Paper money was printed
and Franklin's *Articles of Union* were discussed. In October a
virtual ultimatum was sent to the Canadians, inviting their cooperation or the prospect of an invasion – this was duly launched.
Congress published a *Declaration of the Causes and Necessity*

for taking up Arms drawn up by Jefferson and John Dickinson in order to justify resistance to the Crown:

Our cause is just. Our Union is perfect . . . The arms which we have been compelled by our enemies to assume we will in defiance of every hazard . . . employ for the preservation of our liberties; being with our one mind resolved to die free men rather than live slaves.

Defiant, yet still nominally prepared to be conciliatory, Congress was determined not to avoid war for the sake of an unsatisfactory peace. Dickinson still believed that petitions would bring a favourable response from the king, yet that from the First Congress had been ignored and this second attempt suffered a similar fate. In August Congress rejected Lord North's Conciliatory Proposals and later in 1775 it formed the nucleus of a Foreign Office and authorized the creation of an American navy. Even so the word 'independence' was distrusted and radicals feared to use it in case they forfeited public support. For months on end when it was clear that Britain was preparing to crush the rebellion, Congress failed to be bold in guiding opinion in this matter. Lip service was paid to the honesty of the king, and procrastination in revaluing his part in the crisis threatened to bring dire results if the colonies were not wholly prepared for war.

Three events in London clarified the situation. The first was the Royal Proclamation in August which recognized for the first time that the colonies had rebelled. It demanded that all Britons should cooperate to suppress the rebellion and bring the traitors to justice. Secondly, there was the king's speech to Parliament in October:

The rebellious war now levied is become more general and is manifestly carried on for the purpose of establishing an independent empire.

George was blunter in such matters than the rebels! He also promised that 'decisive exertions' would be taken to put a speedy end to the disorders.

Thirdly, there was the Prohibitory Act of December which ended American trade, making all their goods liable to confiscation, and created a condition of outlawry. This was the harshest act yet and was a declaration of total war. The Americans now had no choice if they wished to save face.

[17] CAUSES OF THE AMERICAN WAR

Underlying the more obvious causes of discontent which led to war was the fact of a maturing American society. This was an inevitable process given the background of the immigrants, the degree of freedom recognized in colonial charters and the lack of interference by Britain in internal matters prior to 1763. The tensions following the Seven Years' War made the propertied class more aware of the need for political action to protect their way of life. Although it is impossible to call the Americans a nation in 1775, yet they had shared common experiences at the hands of successive British governments which threatened them all. Americans rightly believed that their ancestors had developed the land, conquered the Indians and extended their settlements with their own blood and toil. Rugged individualism had created wealth out of a wilderness. Now that this way of life was threatened by an absentee authority with its grasping Treasury and crooked customsmen, opposition crystallized.

American society was also more secure after 1763. Since the earliest days of colonization fears of attack had been omnipresent. French, Dutch and Spaniards threatened the coastal settlements in particular; Indian trouble occurred everywhere and made all colonists, men, women and children into soldiers in self-defence. After 1763 the European threat was extinguished and superior firearms could contain the Indian in all except frontier areas. The defeat of France was as much a climax in American affairs as the destruction of the Spanish Armada of 1588 in English political life; the protestations of the House of Commons in the early seventeenth century were due in no small measure to a sense of security.

A third underlying feature was the growing divergence in the nature of Britain and the American colonies. The historian Charles Andrews pointed to this:

On one side there was the immutable, stereotyped system of the mother country, based on precedent and tradition and designed to keep things comfortably as they were; on the other a vital dynamic organism, containing the seed of a great nation, its forces untried, still to be proved. It is inconceivable that a connection should have continued long between two such yoke fellows, one static, the other dynamic, separated by an ocean and bound only by the ties of a legal relationship.

The ignorance of America on the part of Englishmen has already been described. For their part Americans saw much to fault in British society. Moral, social and political shortcomings were magnified by prejudice and hostile propaganda in press and pamphlet.

The path to war was partly created by the attitude of British ministries. By an imperial policy after 1763 in seeking not only to regulate trade but to raise revenue, the government sought to alter the traditional relationship with the colonies. This destroyed the balance which had existed before 1763 and which seemed to be restored between 1770 and 1773. The American colonies were immensely important to the British economy, and by tightening their control over colonial affairs successive ministries put trade and manufacturing into jeopardy. New policies were therefore withdrawn in 1766 and 1770, but in 1775 public opinion believed that the Americans were unreasonable, so Lord North felt sufficiently confident to proceed rather than withdraw.

British policy was based on three assumptions: first, the need for the mercantile system (which Americans conceded); second, the fairness of colonial taxation to meet colonial expenditure (which most Americans believed to be a denial of their rights); third, the ultimate authority of the Crown in Parliament (about which Americans were unhappy). Lord North did not wish to be tyrannical and George III was no ogre, but they did insist on exercising authority in 1775. War was not willed but was a possible consequence of such a policy. Their actions must be seen in the context of twelve years' friction in American affairs. Neither North nor the king were renowned for perceptive powers above the average, but the situation in 1775 needed such insight. Naturally they expected to win any war which followed; to be firm was not foolhardy when backed by an experienced army and navy.

The American reaction to British policy also led to war.

Colonial grievances are listed in the Declaration of Independence
(on pages 124–7). They may be summarized under two main head-
ings: a refusal to submit to arbitrary government, and fear of a
standing army in time of peace. Many families had come to the
New World during the reigns of Charles I and II and James II
when the threat of tyranny in England supposedly loomed large.
They fled to achieve freedom from persecution; their descendants
were not prepared to succumb meekly. Internal taxation of the
colonies without representation in Parliament, and the shiftiness
of the law seemed to be evidence of arbitrary government. Parliament's refusal to listen to their moderate proposals encouraged
the extremists. All their worst fears were realized in the Coercive
Acts. Even then the majority wanted home rule rather than
independence.

Fear of a standing army was also inherited from England
where the excesses of the Commonwealth had bred a healthy
distaste for soldiers at the right hand of the government. The
Mutiny Act of 1765 and the later reinforcement of Boston were
regarded as a direct assault on colonial freedom, as was the
Quartering Act of 1774. For Americans the true army was the
local militia with its complement of lads electing their own officers
and serving only in their own locality. So strong was the suspicion
of a standing army that during the war Washington had the
greatest difficulty in raising a Continental Army to serve Congress.

Specific causes for complaint existed in all parts of the colonies.
Denial of access to the western lands through the Proclamation
Act of 1763 and the Quebec Act of 1774 struck hard at frontiersman and land speculator alike. It even seemed possible that the
Mississippi valley might find its way into the possession of the
ruling clique in London. Merchants and planters were anxious to
be rid of their debts, but without much prospect of ever achieving
their objective. The hard money demands of the 1764 Currency
Act did not improve their lot. Property was threatened everywhere. For the religious, the problem of bishops in the Episcopal
church was significant, either because they were denied, or because they were abhorred. Everyone wondered whether the
British government was too soft on papists.

Certain radical elements welcomed the opportunity of a civil war to gain home rule and an extension of democracy. Class distinctions were fierce in, for example, New York where the struggle with Britain was paralleled by a conflict between tory property owners and the radicals. The organization of popular opinion gave an impetus to aggression. Both the Sons of Liberty and the Committees of Correspondence advocated extreme methods and were impatient of restraint. Newspapers fed the fires of discontent, and the improved frequency of the mails aided cohesion. Of all the American leaders, only Sam Adams was a true revolutionary. Many moderates assumed positions of leadership through fear of democracy or when the British government showed itself unreasonable.

It is impossible to state which was the crucial factor leading to war: self-interest, home rule, class struggles, British inadequacies, and American maturity are all interrelated. At least the nineteenth-century theory of an evil Britain opposed to a good America seems now to be wildly unhelpful.

Historians have failed to agree about the reasons which led to the American war. 'We must continue to ask, for we still do not fully know, what the Revolution was', wrote Edmund Morgan in a review of changing interpretations of the American Revolution. Indeed, there is a tendency to deny that there was a revolution at all, either political or social. In a very brief survey of this problem, three groups of twentieth-century historians will be used to illustrate some of the different approaches possible.

First, there is the 'imperialist' school of historians, led by George Beer, then Charles Andrews and lately by L. H. Gipson, whose tenth volume on *The British Empire before the American Revolution* (Knopf) appeared in 1961. Professor Gipson argues that British taxation of America was fair, and the fear that taxation without representation would lead to slavery was without foundation. This approach stresses the vacillation in American arguments 1763–75, gives a fairer hearing to the objectives of British policy and apportions responsibility for war more onto the colonists. The weakness of this group is that it has examined the evidence before 1763 in greater depth than for the subsequent period, leaving too much so far unexplained.

Social views of the Revolution are advanced by Carl Becker who in 1909 investigated the political parties in New York colony. He saw the war as a struggle for home rule and who should rule when independence was achieved. In New York he noted the different interests of the old aristocratic families and the popular leaders. Arthur Schlesinger Sr illustrated the Becker view with a study of the relationship between merchants and the radicals (1918). J. F. Jameson (1926) saw the war as the beginning of a democratic upheaval which altered the whole shape of American society. For him it was unquestionably a successful revolution. Charles Beard in *An Economic Interpretation of the Constitution* (Macmillan, 1913) also saw the whole period in terms of class conflict. For him it was a revolution which had failed; the aristocrats of 1775 were the makers of the Constitution of 1787; wealth had triumphed over democracy.

The third group of historians is the modern school which undertakes a more thorough exploration of available material without wishing to prove any major thesis. They share a general dislike of the glibness of some earlier solutions, and are aware of the complexity of the problem with its regional differences. Robert E. Brown attacked the idea of the war as a class conflict. He showed that Massachusetts experienced no democratic revolution because it was democratic before the Revolution began. Studies by other historians of Maryland and New Jersey fail to reveal a social revolution. Brown debunked Beard in his *Charles Beard and the Constitution* (Oxford University Press, 1956), as did F. McDonald in *We The People* (Cambridge University Press, 1959). F. Tolles attacked Jameson's view of a social revolution in the *American Historical Review Vol LX* (1954). The monograph is predominant and investigation of limited topics has produced fine scholarship: O. M. Dickerson's *The Navigation Act and the American Revolution* (University of Pennsylvania Press, 1951) and Edmund Morgan's *Stamp Act Crisis* (University of North Carolina Press, 1953) are examples of this.

So, the study continues, open-ended and stimulating.

Further Reading (1763–75)

Books marked with an asterisk contain more extensive bibliographies which are immensely helpful.

General surveys

*L. H. GIPSON, *The Coming of the Revolution*. Harper Torchbooks (paperback) (New York & London, 1954).

J. C. MILLER, *The Origins of the American Revolution*. Little, Brown (New York, 1943 – reissued 1960).

*E. WRIGHT, *Fabric of Freedom 1763–1800*. Macmillan (London, 1961).

Documents

M. JENSEN, 'English Historical Documents' Vol IX, *American Colonial Documents to 1776*. Eyre & Spottiswoode (London, 1955).

S. E. MORISON, *The American Revolution 1764–1788*. Oxford University Press (London, 1923).

MAX BELOFF (ed), *The Debate on the American Revolution 1761–1783*. Black (London, 1949).

Specific aspects of the period

Imperial
C. M. ANDREWS, *Colonial Background of the American Revolution*. Yale University Press (New Haven, Conn., 1931).

Social
D. J. BOORSTIN, *The Americans 1: The Colonial Experience*. Penguin (Harmondsworth, 1965).

Political thought
C. ROSSITER, *Seedtime of the Republic*. Harcourt, Brace (New York, 1953).

Commercial and political
A. M. SCHLESINGER, *The Colonial Merchants and the American Revolution*. Ungar (New York, 1957).

W. H. NELSON, *The American Tory*. Oxford University Press (London, 1961).

Geographical
R. H. BROWN, *Historical Geography of the United States*. Harcourt, Brace (New York, 1948).

English History

B. DONOUGHUE, *British Politics and the American Revolution 1773-5.*
Macmillan (London, 1964).
R. W. HARRIS, *Political Ideas 1760-92.* Gollancz (London, 1963).
L. B. NAMIER, *England in the Age of the American Revolution.* Macmillan (London, 1930).
*J. S. WATSON, *The Reign of George III.* Oxford University Press (London, 1960).
S. MACCOBY, *English Radicalism 1762-1785.* Allen & Unwin (London, 1955).
I. R. CHRISTIE, *Crisis of Empire: Great Britain and the American Colonies 1754-1783.* Arnold (London, 1966).

Biography

ESMOND WRIGHT, *Washington and the American Revolution.* English Universities Press (London, 1957).
M. CUNLIFFE, *George Washington.* Collins (London, 1959); Mentor (paperback) (New York & London, 1960).
BENJAMIN FRANKLIN, *Autobiography.* Oxford University Press 'World's Classics' (London, 1924).
S. K. PADOVER, *Jefferson.* Cape (London, 1942); Mentor (paperback) (New York & London, 1964).
MAX BELOFF, *Jefferson and American Democracy.* English Universities Press (London, 1948).
J. H. PLUMB, *Chatham.* Collins (London, 1953).

Pamphlet

*E. S. MORGAN, *The American Revolution: A Review of Changing Interpretations.* American Historical Association (1958).

PART IV
The American Revolution

[18] 'COMMONSENSE'

There was no formal declaration of war between the American colonies and Great Britain. How could there be when this was a civil war, a domestic affair, rather than hostilities between two sovereign powers? If Bunker Hill was the first meditated military engagement and the seizure of Ticonderoga and Crown Point an American act of aggression, the political decision to fight was made by the king and embodied in his speech to Parliament in October. Yet before examining the military details it is necessary to trace the movement towards independence, and to account for the position unanimously adopted by the colonies in midsummer 1776.

The most decisive single piece of propaganda was Tom Paine's *Commonsense* published in January 1776. Paine (1737–1809) was born in England and early in life was employed as an excise officer. The service was grossly underpaid and Paine set out his grievances in 1772 in a pamphlet entitled *Case of the Officers of Excise*. Despite its powerful logic and humanity the appeal was ignored by the government, and Paine was dismissed in 1774 for neglect of his duties. This led to a separation from his wife and his sailing to America the same year. He had met Ben Franklin in London and carried letters of introduction to Philadelphia which helped him to find work initially as a teacher, later as a journalist. Paine was well aware of the American political situation in 1775; thoughts of independence were encouraged by such men as Washington, Franklin and Sam Adams while the activities of Congress indicated a drift towards an independent position.

Commonsense was anonymously published and was attributed to the Adamses and Franklin; but the concept and execution belonged to Paine, who drew widely on his English experiences to present an argument which appealed to all sections of American society through its boldness and simplicity. This was the first document to speak out unequivocally for independence – by attacking the British constitution as imperfect, showing George III in a wholly unfavourable light, and exhorting immediate action since the situation demanded separation rather than reconciliation.

His attack upon the king was a novelty. Parliament had already been roundly condemned, all the evils of the day attributed to the mismanagement of the government, but the king had remained untouched. Monarchy, according to Paine, was contrary to the laws of nature and scripture; the principle of hereditary succession was vehemently condemned.

England, since the conquest, hath known some few good Monarchs, but groaned beneath a much larger number of bad ones, yet no man in his senses can say that their claim under William the Conqueror is a very honourable one. A French bastard landing with an armed banditti and establishing himself King of England, against the consent of the natives, is, in plain terms, a very paltry, rascally original.

George III is castigated as the 'Royal Brute of Britain', and in an appendix Paine states that, 'He who hunts the woods for prey, the naked and untutored Indian, is less a savage than the King of Britain'.

Of more worth is one honest man to society, and in the sight of God, than all the crowned ruffians that ever lived.

Indeed, although England had some republican forms, such as the House of Commons, yet the Crown had so corrupted them by its influence that the government was nearly as monarchical as the absolutism of France and Spain.

From this appraisal of the foolishness of monarchy, Paine deduces that independence is the only sensible and practical course for Americans to adopt. Britain had protected the colonies in the past only for the sake of trade and dominion, and these had involved Americans in war. Independence would release them from European involvement and republican government would bring godliness and prosperity. Paine believed independence to be inevitable; now was the time to fight for their children's sake; to withdraw would only lead to greater slavery – 'reconciliation and ruin are nearly related'; American spirits were high; youth and distress gave union against a rich and debased foe; toleration in religion was a good principle by which to stand; resources were boundless, a fleet could be built, debts were no problem. And, very significantly:

It is unreasonable to suppose that France or Spain will give us any kind of assistance, if we mean only to make use of that assistance for the purpose of repairing the breach, and strengthening the connection between Britain and America, because these powers would be sufferers by the consequences.

Foreign aid would be secured only by independence and Paine recommended that a manifesto be circulated to foreign courts to show America's peacable intentions and desire for trade.

The strength of *Commonsense* lay in its bluntness. Politically, it reflected what many had thought but feared to express. It united farmer and merchant who respected its argument and intellectual distinction. Morally, it appealed to instincts of idealism; independence was not just self-seeking, but the establishment of a new republic based on Christian virtue where children could grow in peace. Small wonder, therefore, that circulation of the pamphlet was enormous; among a population of 3 million, 120,000 copies were estimated to have been sold within three months. The effect on Congress was distinctly felt; Charles Lee thought it 'a masterly and irresistible performance', and Washington spoke of 'the sound doctrine and unanswerable reasoning'. By the middle of May Congress was adding the name of the king to that of parliament in the indictment for crimes against the American people. The doctrines of *Commonsense* were assisted when news of the act (December 1775) removing the colonies from royal protection was made known. This was indeed independence, but America cut off by Lord North not vice versa. The American reply was to throw open their ports to trade with all the world, except Britain and her colonies. This collapse of the mercantilist system made reconciliation virtually impossible.

Commonsense was also influential in Europe. Its theme helped the radical cause in France and later in South America, as well as winning friends for the American cause. In Paine's own career it was the only writing which brought him popular acclaim. His later works showed the influence of deistic thought or radical social reform far beyond the comprehension and sympathy of most men of his times. Controversy and calumny were his lot. *The Rights of Man* (1790–2), a reply to Burke's criticism of the French Revolution, and *The Age of Reason* (1793–4) were more profound in many aspects, but *Commonsense* influenced the life of a nation in a way they did not. Independence would have occurred without *Commonsense*; but its publication smoothed the way.

[19] THE PROBLEM OF INDEPENDENCE

Yet why were the colonists so hesitant in declaring their independence?

In the first place the ties of loyalty were immensely strong. Although most Americans were no longer wholly British in blood, and certainly not British in customs or outlook, yet the foundations of their society were undeniably British. To declare independence would be to deny this birthright. Also, Britain had generally behaved well towards her colonies, especially by comparison with other European powers; minimum coercion had been employed and the terrible indictments alleged by the patriots were simply not true as far as the majority of colonists were concerned. Even at this late hour Americans believed that the government would be reasonable. They pinned great faith in the Peace Commissioners, the two Howe brothers, who were reputed to be on their way in the spring of 1776. Their powers were so limited that they could only accept the submission of the colonies. No authority was given them to negotiate a settlement which would satisfy demands for political and economic liberty. Loyalists used the Commission to attempt a postponement of any decision on independence, but as time wore on a general scepticism prevailed. The king did not approve the Howes' appointment until May and by then it was too late to be effective.

A second feature of American hesitation was the weakness of her preparations for war. Congress had taken steps to initiate forms of government, such as raising an independent army, drawing up a code of military law, appointing Indian commissioners, a postal service, and the printing of paper money in addition to the foreign office and navy already mentioned. Yet all these were in a very primitive form early in 1776. They could hardly be called an efficient machine with which to challenge the mighty British Empire. Joseph Hewes wrote:

It is a melancholly fact that near half our men, cannon, muskets, powder, cloathes etc., is to be found nowhere but on paper. We are not discouraged at this; if our situation was ten times worse I would not agree to give up our cause.

Others were not so brave.

A third reason for hesitation was the future relationship with European powers. In the event of independence, many loyalists believed they would be forced to ally with France or Spain, or both. This could mean that on the defeat of Britain America would pass under the control of these Catholic and despotic powers, so that the eventual outcome would be slavery ten times more oppressive than the situation in 1775. A parallel with Poland was drawn. In 1772 Prussia, Austria and Russia had parcelled out some of her territory between them. On the whole this argument was far-fetched, especially when distance from Europe was considered.

Of greater importance were the divisions within America, which independence could bring into prominence. There was the sectional controversy, the distinction between North and South,

East and West. Although recent events had forged a union between the sections this was fragile and the future unpredictable.
Southern planters distrusted the motives of New Englanders;
western farmers never drank tea and did not feel the urge to join
a tea war for the sippers and suppers of New York.

Perhaps even stronger than sectional feeling were class fears.
Some believed that independence would unleash the mob and
democratic government would result in the abolition of wealth
and privilege. In Virginia the old families saw their political
future best assured in the maintenance of British rule, despite
the debts they owed to London merchants. In Philadelphia
Joseph Galloway was said to have 'feared the tyranny of mob rule
more than the tyranny of Parliament'. Colonial society was not
democratic, and the arguments used against the British government could be equally well employed against the 'aristocracy'.
In the event this did not happen. Even the radical Sam Adams
did not want to extend voting rights to all people, and John
Adams believed that to broaden the franchise would in fact
destroy the work of the Revolutionary War. Political whigs
generally were not social revolutionaries. They did not intend to
destroy the hierarchy, but, by ousting the tories, to inherit the
positions of power for themselves. They believed that they could
control the mob, and subsequent history has partially justified
this optimism. The struggle for democracy in America has been
a tough one ever since.

Finally, Congress was delayed in any proclamation on independence by lack of instructions from the various colonies. Although individual delegates might approve, they could not openly
declare themselves until they received a mandate from their local
assembly. North Carolina spoke out plainly in April and in the
next two months the vast majority of colonies followed suit. In
May, Virginia called on Congress to declare independence and in
June a committee including Jefferson, Franklin and John Adams
was appointed to draft a formal declaration.

How had the hesitancy been overcome? Probably the overwhelming factor was the failure of the British government to
show any desire for reconciliation. Lord North's policy to wage

war was put into execution and the belief that Americans had now to be defeated was commonly accepted in England. Any return to the situation of 1763 was now unrealistic. The Prohibitory Bill of December 1775 was regarded as a grant of independence to the colonies – Hewes believed that 'nothing is now left but to fight it out'.

The British cause was not helped by the news that European mercenaries were to be used in America. Russian soldiers were denied by Catherine, but the engagement of German troopers caused emotional panic. These were seasoned veterans and showed that the government meant to subdue rebellion at all costs. Rumour also had it that Negroes and Indians would be used by the British. Unfortunately the activity of Lord Dunmore, royal governor of Virginia, supported this belief. In 1775 he had used Negro slaves to protect the administration, thereby creating the atmosphere of racial war, and the belief that Britain favoured the emancipation of the slaves and Negro domination in the South.

These events were probably more important than the publication of *Commonsense*. Politically, the very slow drift towards independence helped the radicals because it gave no chance for tories to claim that the colonies were being hustled into ill-considered decisions. Increasingly the tories were suspected of disloyalty, and their rising in North Carolina in February 1776 strengthened the patriot contention that a declaration of independence alone would distinguish who were one's friends and who one's enemies. Those who felt this most strongly were often in colonies where British troops had already operated – so the middle colonies were more reluctant to cast adrift than New England. But by June the old colonial system was discarded – Americans replaced British judicial and executive officers, and the colonial assemblies assumed power in their own right, independent of the king.

Congressmen generally agreed that the declaration should be
made on behalf of all the colonies. Delegates from the middle
colonies were, however, uncertain and New York did not give its
approval until 9 July to the momentous decisions made earlier
in the month. On 2 July Congress dissolved the union between
Great Britain and the colonies; on 4 July approval was given to
the Declaration of Independence.

The text is worth giving in full for two reasons; first, for its
statement on the political rights of all mankind. The belief of
Jefferson was a product of the eighteenth-century Enlightenment,
that government belonged to the people and was needed to
secure basic human rights. This is profoundly democratic and
revolutionary by implication. Secondly, the list of grievances
against the king completes Paine's work. It is a practical justification for the American position, although it is a partisan cata-
logue attributing to the king motives to which not even he
subscribed.

THE DECLARATION OF INDEPENDENCE

4 July 1776

The unanimous Declaration of the thirteen United States
of America

When in the course of human events, it becomes necessary for one
people to dissolve the political bands which have connected them with
another, and to assume among the powers of the earth the separate
and equal station to which the Laws of Nature and of Nature's God
entitle them, a decent respect to the opinions of mankind requires
that they should declare the causes which impel them to the separation.

We hold these truths to be self-evident, that all men are created
equal, that they are endowed by their Creator with certain unalienable
rights, that among these are life, liberty, and the pursuit of happiness.

That to secure these rights, governments are instituted among men, deriving their just powers from the consent of the governed. That whenever any form of government becomes destructive of these ends, it is the right of the people to alter or to abolish it, and to institute new government, laying its foundation on such principles and organizing its powers in such form, as to them shall seem most likely to effect their safety and happiness. Prudence, indeed, will dictate that governments long established should not be changed for light and transient causes; and accordingly all experience hath shown, that mankind are more disposed to suffer, while evils are sufferable, than to right themselves by abolishing the forms to which they are accustomed. But when a long train of abuses and usurpations, pursuing invariably the same object evinces a design to reduce them under absolute despotism, it is their right, it is their duty, to throw off such government, and to provide new guards for their future security. Such has been the patient sufferance of these colonies; and such is now the necessity which constrains them to alter their former systems of government. The history of the present King of Great Britain is a history of repeated injuries and usurpations, all having in direct object the establishment of an absolute tyranny over these States. To prove this, let facts be submitted to a candid world.

He has refused his assent to laws, the most wholesome and necessary for the public good.

He has forbidden his Governors to pass laws of immediate and pressing importance, unless suspended in their operation till his assent should be obtained; and when so suspended, he has utterly neglected to attend to them.

He has refused to pass other laws for the accommodation of large districts of people, unless those people would relinquish the right of representation in the legislature, a right inestimable to them and formidable to tyrants only.

He has called together legislative bodies at places unusual, uncomfortable, and distant from the depository of their public records, for the sole purpose of fatiguing them into compliance with his measures.

He has dissolved representative houses repeatedly, for opposing with manly firmness his invasions on the rights of the people.

He has refused for a long time, after such dissolutions, to cause others to be elected; whereby the legislative powers, incapable of annihilation, have returned to the people at large for their exercise;

the State remaining in the meantime exposed to all the dangers of invasion from without and convulsions within.

He has endeavoured to prevent the population of these States; for that purpose obstructing the laws for naturalization of foreigners; refusing to pass others to encourage their migration hither, and raising the conditions of new appropriations of lands.

He has obstructed the administration of justice, by refusing his assent to laws for establishing judiciary powers.

He has made judges dependent on his will alone, for the tenure of their offices, and the amount and payment of their salaries.

He has erected a multitude of new offices, and sent hither swarms of officers to harass our people, and eat out their substance.

He has kept among us, in times of peace, standing armies without the consent of our legislatures.

He has affected to render the military independent of and superior to the civil power.

He has combined with others to subject us to a jurisdiction foreign to our constitution, and unacknowledged by our laws; giving his assent to their acts of pretended legislation:

For quartering large bodies of armed troops among us:

For protecting them, by a mock trial, from punishment for any murders which they should commit on the inhabitants of these States:

For cutting off our trade with all parts of the world:

For imposing taxes on us without our consent:

For depriving us in many cases of the benefits of trial by jury:

For transporting us beyond seas to be tried for pretended offences:

For abolishing the free system of English laws in a neighbouring Province, establishing therein an arbitrary government, and enlarging its boundaries so as to render it at once an example and fit instrument for introducing the same absolute rule into these Colonies:

For taking away our Charters, abolishing our most valuable laws, and altering fundamentally the forms of our governments:

For suspending our own Legislatures, and declaring themselves invested with power to legislate for us in all cases whatsoever.

He has abdicated government here, by declaring us out of his protection and waging war against us.

He has plundered our seas, ravaged our coasts, burnt our towns, and destroyed the lives of our people.

He is at this time transporting large armies of foreign mercenaries to compleat the works of death, desolation, and tyranny, already begun with circumstances of cruelty and perfidy scarcely paralleled in the most barbarous ages, and totally unworthy the head of a civilized nation.

He has constrained our fellow citizens taken captive on the high seas to bear arms against their country, to become the executioners of their friends and brethren, or to fall themselves by their hands.

He has excited domestic insurrections amongst us, and has endeavoured to bring on the inhabitants of our frontiers the merciless Indian savages, whose known rule of warfare is an undistinguished destruction of all ages, sexes, and conditions.

In every stage of these oppressions we have petitioned for redress in the most humble terms: our repeated petitions have been answered only by repeated injury. A prince whose character is thus marked by every act which may define a tyrant, is unfit to be the ruler of a free people.

Nor have we been wanting in attention to our British brethren. We have warned them from time to time of attempts by their Legislature to extend an unwarrantable jurisdiction over us. We have reminded them of the circumstances of our emigration and settlement here. We have appealed to their native justice and magnanimity, and we have conjured them by the ties of our common kindred to disavow these usurpations, which would inevitably interrupt our connections and correspondence. They too have been deaf to the voice of justice and of consanguinity. We must, therefore, acquiesce in the necessity, which denounces our separation, and hold them, as we hold the rest of mankind, enemies in war, in peace friends.

We, therefore, the Representatives of the United States of America, in General Congress assembled, appealing to the Supreme Judge of the world for the rectitude of our intentions, do, in the name, and by authority of the good people of these Colonies, solemnly publish and declare, That these United Colonies are, and of right ought to be Free and Independent States; that they are absolved from all allegiance to the British Crown, and that all political connection between them and the State of Great Britain is and ought to be totally dissolved; and that as Free and Independent States they have full power to levy war, conclude peace, contract alliances, establish commerce, and to do all other acts and things which independent States may of right do. And for the support of this declaration, with a firm reliance on the protection of Divine Providence, we mutually pledge to each other our lives, our fortunes and our sacred honour.

The original draft of the Declaration contained two references which were removed during Congressional debate. A strong censure upon the people of Britain was felt to be impolitic, if not unfair, although a testy indictment of their deafness to pleas for justice remains in the last but one paragraph. More significantly a condemnation of the slave trade was omitted. This was to avoid offence to Southern delegates but also, Jefferson noted at the time, to avoid the embarrassment of Northerners, some of whom earned considerable sums as merchants in the trade.

Originality has not been claimed for this document. Only in its beautifully phrased passages dealing with human rights and the nature of government does it achieve distinction. In dealing with ideas of equality the Declaration betrayed limitations. It is nowhere evident that these rights of life, liberty and the pursuit of happiness applied to the 600,000 slaves; indeed the idea was abhorrent to Congressmen. Nor was the equality of man and woman implied. In terms of economic equality the document was unhelpful. Within American society of 1776 it was obvious that men were not born equal and real power was obtained by means other than human rights or merits. Property qualification and religious tests still existed in most colonies and continued to exercise considerable influence. Only recently have literacy tests designed to bar Negro voters been declared illegal, so the struggle for equality of opportunity must be seen as a continuing one.

This does not detract from the idealistic message which the Declaration contained for future generations. In a world of monarchy and privilege it showed that America was both republican and prepared to be egalitarian; in a world of imperial, traditional values it proclaimed ideals of national determination and democracy; in a Christian context it showed the possibility of the Good Life here and now; in a world of poverty and disease it gave hope that man could conquer his environment and, given the right to the pursuit of happiness, could be profoundly successful.

[21] PREPAREDNESS FOR WAR

Of the three wars which Britain fought in the second half of the eighteenth century, the one in America was singularly disastrous. A lack of vigour characterized the efforts made; there was no Elder Pitt ruthlessly to dictate, no fear of revolutionary subversion which so successfully stirred the upper crust in 1793. In 1776 both France and Spain, who later joined the war against Britain, had sufficient money and large enough fleets to wreak untold damage on the traditional foe. Britain was isolated; the Bourbon powers were without other commitments or enemies.

The British government was ill fitted to wage war under Lord North; he was a peaceful fellow who commanded respect in military and naval circles only as a politician. Nor was the king a leader of ability; his trust in North to win the war was misplaced, his efforts to appoint dynamic ministers were meagre. The leadership in most other departments was equally suspect. The Cabinet, of eight or nine chief ministers, often sheltered behind the façade of collective responsibility. Decisions were executed by the Secretaries of State, but the men who ran both the Northern and the Southern Department were nonentities, and the American war was generally left to the Secretary for the American Colonies, Lord George Germain.

Germain (1716–85) – he changed his name from Sackville in 1770 to inherit a fortune – is a controversial figure. Traditionally much maligned, he is an enigmatic character but with many redeeming features. Essentially a soldier, his career before 1775 was a tale of courage but apparent disgrace. His relationship with General Wolfe was friendly and fellow officers confirmed his ability and character. In 1759 at the battle of Minden in Germany he was slow to the attack with his cavalry in support of Ferdinand of Brunswick. Dismissed from the Army he sought a court-martial, which was reluctantly given him, and he was found guilty of disobedience, not of cowardice, which is commonly reputed to be the charge. Humiliated in addition by George II, he expected and obtained better things from George III and Lord

Bute, regaining his place on the Privy Council together with minor office. In 1775 he contributed useful qualities of determination and experience to the Administration, although he remained vulnerable to the Minden incident. In particular he had powerful enemies in the Secretary at War, Lord Barrington, who had arranged his court martial, and the Earl of Sandwich, First Lord of the Admiralty. His personal failings included obstinacy and arrogance; his political shortcomings, the lack of a following in the House of Commons, or the genius of a Pitt in making a war machine spin along.

The navy was the most important department of the British war machine. An island's safety depends on her ability to control the seas, and in the American war Britain lost this supremacy for the only time in modern history. The Admiralty provided not only warships but transports, dockyards, storehouses, supply lines and a system of recruitment. Power over this complex system was exercised by the Lords Commissioners of the Admiralty with the Earl of Sandwich (1718–92) as First Lord. He was a notorious rake who had bitterly offended radicals by his persecution of his friend John Wilkes, a fellow member of the Monks of Medmenham 'sect', and who was fair game for the righteous through the looseness of his morals. Sandwich had a mistress, Martha Ray, who bore him two children, but she was shot in 1779 by a young clergyman who had wished to marry her. Succeeding to the First Lordship in 1771, an immensely important post of patronage best seen in the seventeen votes which he controlled in the House of Commons, Sandwich was bitterly attacked after 1775 for failing to provide an adequate fleet; yet the Treasury was much to blame. In the attempt to keep taxation low and to balance the budget, only limited money was available for maintenance let alone new building. Deficiencies in naval provisioning did not become crucial until the entry of France into the war in 1778, but by 1779 France and Spain could muster 140 capital ships to the 123 of the Royal Navy.

The more immediate task of conquest in America lay with the army. George III took an intense personal interest in its welfare and controlled its patronage. The Secretary at War was not an

influential politician or military leader, so the appointment of
Lord Amherst as commander-in-chief in 1778 was long overdue.
The generals, such as Howe and Burgoyne, were men with influential social connections, most often with the nobility. They
were anxious to improve their lot, and personal ambition was
sometimes more in evidence than concern for the national interest
or their men. Lower in the scale commissions were invariably
bought. This aristocratic hierarchy often soldiered well through
long experience and personal courage rather than intellectual
power or formal training. Appalling inadequacies did appear,
however – one of Howe's regiments was commanded by a colonel
so overcome with gout that he could barely walk; another was
nominally commanded by a lunatic. No one emerged from the
American war with military credit. Marlborough, Wolfe and
Wellington were all products of the same system but Howe,
Clinton and Amherst were without imaginative genius. Only
Cornwallis seemed likely to emerge with a worthy reputation, and
even he was humbled by the surrender at Yorktown.

The British Army was 27,000 strong in infantry and cavalry
in 1775, and this rose to 150,000 by 1782. Many troops enlisted
to gain employment, especially in Scotland where economic conditions were most tough, but the life was not attractive and recruitment was often by dubious means. Bribery, drink and an
alternative to prison sentences were all legitimate means of
raising a regiment. Small wonder, therefore, that discipline was
harsh. 1,000 lashes with the cat o'-nine tails was sometimes given
for serious offences, 300 often for a misdemeanour; minor punish-
ments included clubbing, 'Removal to the Navy' or service in
the West Indies where the mortality rate through disease was so
high.

British troops in North America were the most difficult to
supply. By February 1778 there were 50,000 soldiers to be kept
alive. The countryside yielded less than expected, though local
dealers shrewdly raised prices for the occasion. The bulk of the
provisions came from Britain, and Cork in southern Ireland was
the main base. Hazards plagued the whole system; the quality of
rations was suspect, packing was inadequate, thieving and ad-

ministrative delay all too common. Campaigning suffered as a
result. In 1776 Howe had to delay his departure from Halifax
prior to the attack on New York because of the lateness of the
arrival of provision ships. Throughout his 1777 campaign, too,
he was less mobile than expected because of similar difficulties.
Not only British troops served in North America. So demanding
was the scope of the war that mercenaries and auxiliaries had to
be employed: 29,000 German professional troops served the
Crown; they were tough and disciplined if rather inflexible in
their attitudes. Conditions in America were different from European battlefields, and the necessary transition in tactics was not
always made. Without these troops Britain could not have met
her worldwide commitments – in Ireland, the Mediterranean,
India and the West Indies, not to mention the need to defend
England herself from invasion. The Germans struck fear into
patriot hearts, but so did the Indians who also inspired hatred
since their rules of war did not respect women and children. Their
value was marginal because they were so unreliable. Of much
more importance than Indians were the loyalist volunteers. The
Canadians were particularly welcome, but Howe all too often
discouraged the New England tories from volunteering, distrust-
ing their military capacity as well as their political motives. Their
numbers never rose over 8,200 men.

The American army was a very different affair. Its officers were
hardly of the nobility, although Washington was a patrician.
Both Charles Lee and Horatio Gates had served in the British
army, but Washington had held rank only in the militia. When
he was appointed Commander-in-Chief he had Artemus Ward of
New England and Lee directly under him, with Gates as Adjutant-
General, a fair sprinkling of experience although the British at
first preferred to believe that the American army contained only
Irishmen and recent immigrants. Recruits were experienced only
so far as they had seen service in the militia during the Seven
Years' War or had experience in shooting game or Indians, a task
which demanded considerable skills of marksmanship.

Local militia units had existed for many years but by the
1770s were poorly led and by no means coordinated. Stocks of

munitions ran low and a lack of uniformity in equipment caused confusion; rifles lacked bayonets and the cannon was likely to blow up in the gunner's face. Yet morale was initially high. Enlistment for service outside the home area never became popular, and the period of service was short, usually for one to three months. Certainly at the beginning of the War there was no conception of a 'Continental Army', indeed many feared a standing army even in time of war as a threat to individual liberty. Washington had to create his Continental Army and his achievement in so doing cannot be underestimated; it proved to be the one reliable fighting force which kept in the field.

Conditions for both militia and Continentals were poor. Benjamin Thompson wrote that the army was 'wretchedly clothed and as dirty a set of mortals as ever disgraced the name of soldier'. Men enlisted voluntarily rather than by draft, some through loyalty or material reward or just forced to do so by local pressures. Free Negroes, but not slaves, served in the army although this was not popular in the South. Discipline could be haphazard and insubordination rife. Privates were known to select their commanders and considered themselves socially their equals or superiors. Desertion was common, especially to return to the farms.

'Some have got a great quantity of grass to cut; some have not finished hoeing corn . . . it is enough to make a man's heart ache to hear the complaints of some of them', wrote Colonel Fitch of Connecticut. Washington's force at Valley Forge 1777–8 dropped from 17,000 to 5,000 men, mainly through desertion.

In 1776 Congress appointed a War board, five Congressmen to acquire provisions and oversee the war. A munitions factory was established, but the firearm situation remained serious until French supplies arrived. In July 1776 it was reckoned that a quarter of the army had no arms, and that Saratoga in 1777 was won with French weapons. Rivalry was also apparent between the claims of individual States (the term 'colony' is hardly applicable after the Declaration of Independence), Congress and the Commander-in-Chief. Confusion was only avoided later by giving Washington almost dictatorial power. There was no guarantee that any American army would perform in a predictable fashion; the composition of each army and the quality of commanders seemed so variable that the sheer discipline of British troops might have been expected to win the day.

It should now be possible to construct a balance sheet, looking at the advantages of both armies in the autumn of 1775.

Britain had the advantage of a historical record of success in the eighteenth century. From Blenheim to the Peace of Paris she had won her way when threatened, not without cost (the National Debt stood at £163 million in 1775) but with the accession of a world-wide empire. Her reputation was immense, so great of course that her European rivals eagerly waited for a chance to clip her wings. Her navy was the largest in Europe, her troops were loyal and she was known to produce heroes fit for any occasion. There was no reason to suggest that in 1775 her army and navy would be less than successful against an American foe. The early history of the war, indeed, confirmed that the initiative lay with Britain. Unity of command was undermined by personal rashness or muddle but in 1775 the potential organization for war gave the British an undeniable advantage.

In full-scale battle conditions the Americans were likely to be exceedingly puny. Without a regular army, with discipline and coordination suspect, it is small wonder that the loyalists reckoned that the patriot army was a 'contemptible body of vagrants, deserters and thieves'. It was said that 'English Mastiffs be not scar'd at the Barking of American Curs'. When battle was joined the curs did not behave predictably. At sea there was no American navy. The activities of John Paul Jones were those of a patriotic buccaneer and as such were audacious and successful, causing the government much concern by his raids on the Cumbrian and Yorkshire coasts. Yet until the entry of France the British fleet held mastery of the seas, and would have continued to do so.

Politically, the weakness of the American union gave an advantage to the British. There was no certainty that the agreements of Congress would survive military pressure. In particular there was a possibility that war would detach the southern colonies. Only in New England was there a passionate devotion to the objectives of the war. The tory, or loyalist, element was also supposed to give advantage to the British, but this was never the case. Partly the government lost sympathy by its decisions in late 1775, or by the introduction of mercenaries into America; colonials were inspired by the Declaration of Independence and tories found difficulty in opposing this new national spirit. The expectation of tory assent was reasonable in 1775 even though it eventually proved to be one of the major miscalculations of the war.

Financially, Britain could afford the war. She had the foundation of a sound economy upon which to draw and the country gentry, not without protest, again bore the strain. Taxation soared and was fairly expended upon crucial items; the failure of the war was not so much shortage of cash as tardiness of supply or deployment of equipment. The Americans had to create a financial machine to raise money. Central and local taxation was never popular because it smelt too much of the old British tyranny. Consequently state taxes raised only $6 million in specie before 1784, or less than $2 a head. Vast amounts of paper money were printed by Congress and individual States which led to inflation, a situation aggravated by shortage of goods. Later in the war French and Spanish currency helped to stabilize finance but the war machine was backed by the flimsiest of monetary structures.

Despite these disheartening aspects, the Americans could find several factors in their favour. Probably the most valuable of these was a growing belief in themselves as people who ought of right to be free and independent. They fought to save their homes and families, their way of life and their future. This sense of destiny (for want of a better word) gave immense hope and meant that Americans could never have been denied independence despite any military defeat. The deepest feelings of loyalty were never called upon because the British failed to achieve military supremacy, but one can imagine the impossibility of controlling a civilian population determined to be free. It was commonly believed that the population of America would eclipse that of Britain – 96 million were forecast for 1866 (actually it was 38 million). Franklin was very conscious of this potential growth and had urged Englishmen to nurse America for future generations. Patriots came forward to do battle, and showed qualities of courage and marksmanship which, allied to guerrilla tactics, frustrated British efforts. Reserves of manpower were abundant, whereas the defeat at Saratoga cost Howe 7,000 troops who could not be immediately replaced.

Americans also despised many aspects of British society. It was regarded as decadent. One commentator in 1775 said:

The teeth are harmless, the claws are impotent and this British lion . . . will turn out nothing but a Scottish Ass from the Isle of Bute.

This feeling of superiority was, of course, strengthened after success at Lexington and Bunker Hill.

A second feature of American advantage was geographical. The 3,000-mile passage across the Atlantic took over a month from west to east, and at least two months from London back to America. This created administrative havoc. The British government had never before been called upon to wage a major war so far from home. Regular correspondence was impossible, supplies went astray and all planning was subject to the hazards of nature upon the high seas. Germain recognized that his commanders required discretion in matters of battlefield strategy; London could not dictate orders, but could organize supplies and coordinate plans, or act as a referee for the demands of rival commanders.

Within America itself geography posed insuperable problems. The area to be conquered was so vast it could never be held, or the inhabitants could melt into the west; overland communications, especially between Canada and New York were treacherous as Burgoyne later discovered; ice in the St Lawrence and the heat in the South took their toll of men and efficiency. Local guerrilla troops, such as the Green Mountain Boys in Vermont, used the countryside to excellent advantage; the absence of large cities denied the British the occupation of any decisive centre of resistance. New York, Philadelphia and Charleston were all seized, but still the war went on.

Britain helped the colonists indirectly by refusing to wage total war. Americans were still members of the empire and the object of the war was to restore the relationship with Crown and Parliament through the destruction of revolutionary government. Thus the Howe brothers were Peace Commissioners as well as military commanders, and many troops were unhappy about fighting their own countrymen or using Indians. Towns were occasionally burned, prisoners of war not always well treated, but there was little of the sheer savagery of war such as Sherman's march through Georgia during the Civil War in 1864.

Of inestimable advantage to the Americans was the friendship of European powers. Britain's isolation was complete. Neither France nor Spain was attracted by principles of democracy but both were prepared to go to war against Britain. France in particular played a crucial role; her money, troops and naval power were indispensable. The war was disastrous for her in that she gained little comfort from peace terms and was saddled with a debt which created a desperate financial crisis. Details of foreign alliances will be discussed later.

The advantage of leadership lay with the Americans. Much is written of Washington's excellence but this is more true of personal example, courage and tenacity than military genius. After all, the Americans lost most of the battles fought. Almost trapped on Manhattan in 1776, he learnt slowly from mistakes and certainly met the demands of war as did no one else. His fellow military leaders failed – Arnold deserted to the British, Lee was court-martialled, Ward did not blossom and Gates was defeated in the South. Washington kept an army in the field and, even in 1781 when enthusiasm was fading, he maintained the objectives of war. Time was not necessarily on the side of the patriots, especially if the British fleet could inflict a heavy defeat on the French. In all situations, however, Washington fulfilled the tasks assigned him by Congress. No British general matches his stature. Howe was too slow, Burgoyne too arrogant and selfish, Clinton too stuffy. Admiral Rodney emerges as a popular hero for his victory off the Saints in 1782 but this engagement does not entitle him to rank alongside Washington.

Neither the British nor the Americans could feel confident about the outcome of war in 1775. There were too many imponderables. This was the last war of the Ancien Régime; six years after its completion the French Revolution gave Europe a new ideology, and warfare, with greater technological efficiency, became more ferocious.

[22] MILITARY EVENTS

1775–6

Two areas in North America demanded immediate attention in the autumn of 1775 – Boston and Canada. Following the military setbacks at Lexington and Bunker Hill and considering local hostility, the plight of the garrison in Boston was alarming. Similarly the American advance to Ticonderoga and Crown Point made the towns of Montreal and Quebec vulnerable to attack. It was essential to hold all three centres through the winter and spring 1775–6, so that a confident offensive could be launched in early summer. Only one offensive was planned before then, and proved most unfortunate. This was to aid loyalists in the South. In November a rising in South Carolina had been put down by patriots, and in February 1776 loyalists in North Carolina rose expecting to be supported by troops brought by Clinton from the North. These never arrived so the affair collapsed. Clinton was not ready to act until May and then proceeded to an abortive assault on the fortifications of Charleston. He lost a ship, men and even more important, time, because he should have been in support of Howe's New York summer campaign.

General Howe had assumed command in Boston. He had a garrison of 9,000 men facing Washington's force which was in the process of training. Supplies from England did not arrive – 26 ships were blown off course and ended up in the West Indies – so his situation in early spring was desperate. He could not attack and evacuation by sea was hampered by an insufficient number of transports. Deadlock was broken in March 1776 by the arrival of artillery which the Americans had hauled across New England from Ticonderoga. This was set up on Dorchester Heights, commanding the harbour, so Howe had either to launch an assault or withdraw as swiftly as possible. British strategy included eventual evacuation of Boston, but not in the manner which now became necessary. Valuable stores were abandoned and personnel were stuffed on board ship in a most undignified fashion. On 17 March, St Patrick's Day, much to the delight of Irish patriots, Howe sailed from Boston to Halifax, Nova Scotia.

Events in Canada were more dramatic. Richard Montgomery led 2,000 Americans from Ticonderoga against 800 regular British troops under Guy Carleton. Gradually Carleton fell back. The Americans took Montreal in November and the sudden appearance of Benedict Arnold's army almost led to the fall of Quebec. Arnold had led his men through the exhausting backcountry of Maine to the St Lawrence. Starvation, sickness and desertion had reduced his force of 1,100 to only 500 men. It was a heroic march, but too late. He could not press the attack on the city immediately and volunteer troops kept him out; Carleton, who had been ambushed on his retreat from Montreal, slipped into Quebec, a strongly fortified citadel which the joint force of Arnold and Montgomery failed to take. Montgomery was killed and Arnold was wounded, and when British reinforcements reached the city in May 1776, the tide had turned against the Americans. Hampered by smallpox, desertion and an invigorated foe, they were forced to withdraw.

1776

Having weathered the winter storm, Britain could now undertake major reconquest. Strategy was based upon the Hudson river and the Canada–New York axis. Both the generals and Germain agreed on the soundness of the plan. They aimed to dominate the Hudson through the capture of New York in the south and the advance of an army from Canada in the north.

This was expected to bring three important results: first, it would divide the American forces and isolate New England which would then be attacked by sea through Boston or Newport, Rhode Island; secondly, it would rally loyalists in upper New York State where they were reputedly numerous; thirdly, it would enable Canadian resources to be available to armies in the thirteen colonies. Yet at an early stage plans went awry. The arrival of men or equipment could not be depended upon and the absence of an overall command led to the negation of a basically sound scheme. Already the plan was behind schedule; by spring 1776 Germain had hoped that New York would be taken and the Canadian army already on the upper Hudson. Instead, there were British armies in Halifax and on the St Lawrence, and a year's delay before the strategy clicked into action. According to the initial timetable Saratoga ought to have occurred in 1776!

1776 proved to be a year of jockeying for position and was far less decisive than expected. Howe established an army in New York and its vicinity, Carleton was reinforced in Canada, and an advance was made towards the Hudson, but the enemy remained in the field, intact.

General Howe was delayed in Halifax by a shortage of provisions and could not sail for New York until June. This was already too late in the season for comfort. He landed on Staten Island, at the mouth of New York harbour early in July and sat there for seven weeks before attempting a full assault on Long Island. The delay was wasteful but there was a justification. Howe was concerned for the welfare of his men and was fully aware that they were the nucleus of the fighting force in America. To risk their safety and be other than certain of victory would be to imperil the empire. A hasty commitment to battle without adequate supplies such as landing craft, and even camp kettles, would be criminal folly. He, therefore, waited until August by which time he had received supplies, Guards and Hessian troops, Clinton's regiments from Charleston and his brother Admiral Howe, to command the fleet. By then 25,000 troops were available.

The Americans had not been slow to prepare defences. Charles

Lee had arrived in February to survey the land and begin digging, Washington himself arrived in April and some 20,000 troops were ready. The Declaration of Independence had boosted morale, but had not made the defence of New York any easier. Encircled on so many sides by navigable rivers, with islands complicating the pattern, the city was at the mercy of superior naval forces; the initiative lay with the attack rather than defence. Brooklyn Heights, opposite Manhattan, became the pivot of the American effort. New York had to be defended: it was a great port and arsenal, it controlled the Hudson, and to surrender tamely would encourage loyalists everywhere. At the same time Washington could not afford to commit himself to a decisive battle.

British troops landed unopposed on Long Island. The bulk of the American troops occupied a line to the south of Brooklyn Heights in an attempt to break the British line of advance. They expected a frontal assault as at Bunker Hill, but Howe achieved a flanking movement which completely broke their left. With heavy casualties the Americans retreated in confusion and despair behind their inner fortifications against the East river.

Legitimate criticism can surely be levelled at Howe in these circumstances. His superiority was everywhere apparent. True a north wind denied the navy access to the East River to bar a retreat, but on Long Island initiative lay with the British. Yet Howe, instead of launching an assault on the main position, ordered siege works to be dug. A cooling off period followed in which Washington realized his weakness and withdrew to Manhattan Island under the cover of night and a storm.

On 15 September Howe began his attack on Manhattan and New York city. The landing was a complete success and the patriots were thoroughly disorganized. A chance to cut off several thousand Americans in New York was lost and a retreat to Harlem Heights allowed. Howe had won New York, a fine achievement, but he had not destroyed the enemy army. A month later he renewed the attack. To winkle Washington out of Harlem troops were landed by sea behind American lines. Washington withdrew to White Plains where he skilfully avoided an engagement with Howe at the end of October.

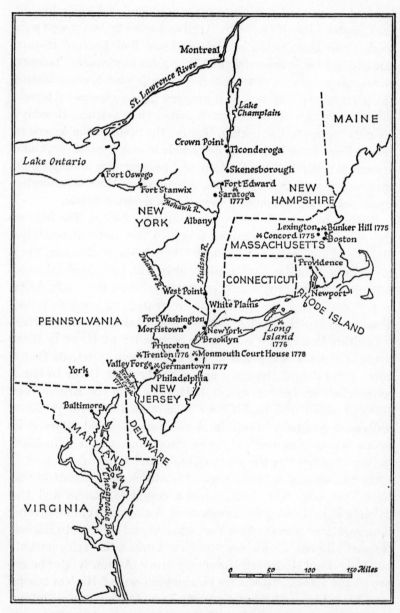

THE WAR 1776–83: *New England and the Middle States*
(*adapted from Muir's Historical Atlas*)

The British then turned westward and completely routed the 3,000 strong garrison at Fort Washington on the Hudson, a major triumph. The fort was believed to be easily defensible. Washington also divided his army – detachments of about 5,000 men dispersing to New Jersey and north up the Hudson river, a third remaining at White Plains. The American cause was in serious decline. Howe certainly showed a more aggressive instinct when he sent Cornwallis into New Jersey. In face of his advance Fort Lee was abandoned and Washington was forced out of New Jersey to the west bank of the Delaware river; New Jersey became loyalist almost to a man. Cornwallis did not attempt the dangerous crossing of the Delaware, and the advent of winter persuaded Howe to halt the offensive and consolidate for a fresh onslaught the following year.

American self-respect was restored by a surprise attack across the Delaware on Boxing Day. The Hessian troops at Trenton were still feeling the effect of Christmas celebrations and were totally unprepared; they broke and fled. Washington was encouraged to continue the attack and return to Trenton on 31 December only to be met by Cornwallis with superior forces. Disaster was avoided by a skilful retreat eastwards to Princeton by night. Here a brush with the redcoats was reckoned to be a patriot victory, and the march was continued north to Morristown where winter quarters were comfortably established. British forces withdrew to quarters not far from Staten Island, abandoning Trenton and eastern New Jersey.

Elsewhere, Clinton had taken Rhode Island at the beginning of December. No difficulty was expected or experienced in this operation which gave the fleet an excellent harbourage, control of Connecticut shipping and a base from which to launch an attack into New England. No attempt was made to press battle up the Hudson.

This theatre of war was redeemed for the Americans by the late recovery. The loss of New York, the Hudson forts and New Jersey seriously undermined enthusiasm for war. The counterstrokes were daringly conceived and were acclaimed as major victories. Neither Trenton nor Princeton ever threatened British military supremacy, but did encourage withdrawal to a small area around New York.

In Canada Carleton had failed to gain as much headway as hoped. Reinforcements from Britain had been sufficient to drive the Americans back to Lake Champlain but that waterway was a major obstacle to his advance on the Hudson. He had no boats and Germain had been unable to supply them in the spring as requested. Therefore he had to set to in midsummer to construct a fleet which could not only destroy the few craft manned by Americans, but would act as transports. Arnold was responsible for American determination to contest the passage of the lake and it was a strategy which paid a handsome dividend. Although Carleton's men worked feverishly to fulfil his orders, he was too cautious in estimating the strength required and spent too long on over-elaborate preparation. Not until October were the ships ready for action, and so strong were they that the result was never in doubt. Crown Point was abandoned and Arnold fell back on Ticonderoga. Yet because winter was approaching Carleton fell back even from Crown Point, without testing the strength of Ticonderoga which was not so healthily guarded as he expected. Carleton failed to show an adventurous spirit in pressing forward and this gave the Americans a chance to strengthen defences on the Hudson and allowed them to enter 1777 without major defeat on the Canadian front.

1776 was a disappointment for British hopes. Her generals had not lost a battle but they had not gained the initiative; the break-through along the Hudson had not materialized, American forces were still intact, and now experienced under fire. The generals had been cautious to the point of folly and Washington had been allowed to escape from New York. Among American successes could be counted the fall of Boston, the defeat of loyalist risings in the Carolinas and the failure of Clinton at Charleston. Washington's selection of Morristown for the winter rather than a retreat into New England upset British calculations; it meant that the Rhode Island base would not be able to engage a major American army. The plan to confine Washington east of the Hudson had broken down.

[23] 1777

The New Year saw Carleton in disgrace in London. Germain was his personal enemy, a relationship which neither man cared to improve. The Governor of Quebec was badly treated by Germain; on the recall of Gage he had been the senior general in America but Howe superseded him. It was Germain's intention even in 1776 that he would be replaced by Clinton or Burgoyne. The Cabinet was not satisfied that he ought to have relinquished Crown Point and the return of John Burgoyne, his second-in-command, to London in December 1776 further damned his reputation. In February 1777 Burgoyne was appointed to lead the expedition from Canada, an odd situation whereby Carleton maintained supreme civil authority in Quebec and responsibility for supplies, but without a say in the disposal of his army. Piers Mackesy believes that 'the choice of Burgoyne was the worst ministerial error of the campaign; perhaps the only avoidable one'.

'Gentleman Johnny' Burgoyne (1722–92) was a man of varied tastes and interests; he was soldier, politician, playwright and man about town. He had eloped with the daughter of the Earl of Derby and always used his family connections with utter ruthlessness. This, combined with bravado and fair military expertise, enabled him to rise rapidly in rank from captain to brigadier and command of a regiment. His relationship with his men was good for the times and his nickname was one of affection. Yet he was bombastic and ill-disciplined, far too ambitious to be personally honest. In 1775 he had joined Gage at Boston, whom he described to the ministry as 'unequal to his present station'. His power was enhanced since he was a member of Parliament and sat for Preston from 1768 to 1792. At his election he had gone to the poll with a guard of soldiers and a loaded pistol in each hand. He was tried for incitement to violence, fined £1,000, but kept his seat.

On 28 February Burgoyne sent Germain a detailed plan of his intended campaign. Basically it was the well-established idea

which had dominated the thinking of 1776, namely the advance
from Canada to the Hudson at Albany where he would place himself under Howe's command. This plan, however, had to be considered in relationship to three communications from General
Howe which reached London between December 1776 and February 1777. The first letter maintained the by now traditional
pattern of the Canadian expedition joining with a force of 10,000
men sent from New York. He called for reinforcements to do this as
well as hold New York and to launch an attack into New England.
A second letter, written on 20 December, but arriving in London
as late as 23 February, took into account the push across New
Jersey; Howe believed Philadelphia would easily fall into his
hands. His attention was therefore now directed south to Pennsylvania, rather than northwards to Albany. The bulk of his
forces was to be used to break Washington around the Congressional capital and an army of 10,000 would not be available to
join Burgoyne on the Hudson. Instead a force of 3,000 regulars
would be left on the lower Hudson to help Burgoyne if needed.
This was a radical change of plan. The third letter was written
after the setback at Trenton and Princeton. More reinforcements
were called for, but the campaign against Philadelphia would
continue.

So, while Burgoyne was still in London and before Carleton's
orders were dispatched, the shift of Howe's interest to Philadelphia was well known and approved by Germain. Burgoyne knew
that he could no longer count on active cooperation from Howe
on the middle reaches of the Hudson, although some troops
would be available in an emergency. The point is that Burgoyne
was confident of success without support from the south and this
arrogance was sustained until the position near Saratoga became
impossible. He severely underestimated both the geographical
advantages afforded to defenders in the wilderness of Vermont,
and the number of patriot troops who would muster to oppose
his 10,000 strong army.

It is clear that Burgoyne knew of Howe's plans. But did Howe
know that Burgoyne was to launch a summer offensive from
Canada? At this point there emerges the story of Germain's

failure to send the necessary letter of instruction to Howe. But no such failure occurred. A copy of Carleton's orders was sent to Howe and acknowledged by him in May. Germain did not send a personal covering note but left this to a friend of Howe, D'Oyly, who failed to keep a copy for the file. Nor did the American Secretary intend to send orders to Howe about Burgoyne's campaign – he had already approved Howe's disposition of troops and Burgoyne was not worried about the overall picture. As usual, Germain trusted his generals in the field to liaise with each other and to consider difficulties as they arose. No attempt was made by London to dictate. Carleton's orders were so specific because Burgoyne had been at hand to give advice and this was the only way to ensure the Governor's full cooperation in a business from which he had been demoted.

It was only in April that Howe again modified the support which he could afford the advance from Canada. The letter reached London in May, too late for Germain to change plans even if he had wished. No longer were 3,000 regulars to be available on the lower Hudson, but 3,000 loyalists, with a garrison of 4,700 regulars in New York itself. Howe promised to have regard for the safety of the Canadian expedition but the underlying assumption was that unless Washington broke off from Philadelphia nothing would prevent Burgoyne from reaching Albany. He wrote to Carleton and Burgoyne explaining this, and the latter does not appear to have been horrified or to have hesitated. This fourth letter was probably more important for the news it contained of his change in plan for the Philadelphia campaign. Abandoning the overland route through New Jersey, he announced the embarkation of an expedition by sea to the mouth of the Delaware river, south of the city.

So, in mid 1777 the strategy resolved itself: deferring an attack from Rhode Island on New England, the spheres of military activity would be Philadelphia and the upper Hudson river.

Philadelphia

Howe had decided against a march across New Jersey because of Washington's position on his right flank and the difficulty in crossing the Delaware. Instead he embarked 15,000 men and baggage with everything ready for sailing on 23 July. Opposition to the move was intense from some of his officers, Clinton in particular. He objected to the loss of all gains in New Jersey for the sake of bringing Washington to battle over Philadelphia, a city which he might well decline to defend.

The army was afloat until 25 August and, instead of landing on the banks of the Delaware, because Howe considered the defences too strong, it landed at the head of Chesapeake Bay, adding 25 days to the voyage and landing as far from Philadelphia as it had been on the day of embarkation. This was hardly the masterly tactical stroke which Howe had hoped to achieve. The condition of his men and horses in the heat and close confines of the ships had deteriorated badly, whereas Washington had had time to complete the muster of his army.

Yet success lay with the British. At the battle of Brandywine Creek the inadequacy of the American forces was plainly revealed. A flanking movement similar to that on Long Island was executed by Cornwallis, but this time sufficient fresh American reserves held the weary British until nightfall. No attempt was made to follow up the victory which saw the Americans falling back in confusion, ripe for the havoc which could have been caused by marauding regulars. After skilful manoeuvering by Howe, the way to Philadelphia lay open and the city was occupied on 25 September. Howe then had to deploy his troops – 3,000 remained in the city, others went to clear the forts along the Delaware, others to bring up further supplies from the Chesapeake, but the bulk of his men, 9,000, he left at Germantown, seven miles from the city. They did not entrench, and the Americans seized the chance of a surprise attack. After a night march of 16 miles Washington launched a dawn offensive on 4 October. Fog confused the picture and the Americans were not sufficiently expert to press their advantage. When Cornwallis brought up reserves, the Continentals fell back.

Events later in the year did not lead to the expulsion of the British from Philadelphia. Nor did they bring Howe any decisive advantage. He ventured an attack on the American position at Whitemarsh in December but withdrew when the extent of the fortifications was known. The Delaware river was cleared of enemy blockades and made free for shipping. Far more decisive were events to the north along the Hudson river.

Saratoga

Burgoyne returned to Quebec from London on 6 May bringing with him Carleton's specific orders as laid down by Germain. Carleton's reaction was predictable – he wrote a stinging letter offering his resignation but was too much of an old soldier to deny Burgoyne every help in preparing the expedition. Organization was much more frustrating than Burgoyne had anticipated; he was short of local patriots and Indians, boats had to be made for his artillery and he was disgusted to find that a paper was circulating in Montreal revealing the full extent of his plans – a security leak.

Simultaneous with Burgoyne's main advance, St Leger with a body of 1,700 men, including Canadians and Indians, was to set out from Fort Oswego on Lake Ontario down to Mohawk Valley to join the main force at Albany. His first obstacle was Fort Stanwix, occupied by 500 Continentals prepared to withstand siege. Initially they could not be winkled out, so St Leger sent troops to bring up cannon and additional supplies. In their absence 800 American reinforcements arrived under General Herkimer to outnumber St Leger. During the engagement General Herkimer was killed, and his troops compelled to withdraw. Nonetheless they had improved the morale of the besieged men and discomforted the Indians. The garrison refused to surrender and awaited relief. This came with Benedict Arnold's column, but the fort was relieved by subtlety not by force. Arnold did not wish to fight. Instead he released a tory spy, a halfwitted fellow whom he had captured, with the promise of freedom, if he would go to St Leger's Indians and report that a vast American army was approaching. Accompanied by a few patriot Indians the crazy man was so successful that the British redskins after looting from their officers, promptly deserted. St Leger, therefore, hurriedly gave up the siege and tried to rejoin Burgoyne via Montreal, but was too late to be of any further assistance. The secondary advance had failed miserably.

Burgoyne set sail on Lake Champlain in late June. In his force of some 9,500 men he had 7,000 regular soldiers including 3,000 Germans. It was a proficient, if small, force with excellent spirits. In addition there was the usual horde of camp women. Ordinary soldiers despatched to America were allowed to take their 'wives' with them, partly to prevent desertion, and both women and children were provided for from public funds. Women were known to have gone on to the field of battle, and certainly children were born on the march. Officers, of course, proved no exception to this homely situation.

Ticonderoga was the first objective. It was expected to be a stiff obstacle and the large number of cannon was shipped with this in mind. In the event little resistance was offered. Burgoyne was able to occupy a 600-foot hill which allowed him to dominate the fort with his guns and the garrison melted away on 5 July. Tremendous excitement spread through the British army at this easy capture and the general believed he could destroy enemy resistance in New England singlehanded.

He pressed southwards with determination to Skenesborough, engaging the enemy rearguard at Hubbardtown, when victory was bought at the cost of 200 casualties. The next objective was Fort Edward, the nearest navigable point on the Hudson river. Either he could return to Ticonderoga and strike south-west along Lake George, then eastwards to the Fort over passable roads, a total of 70 miles; or he could take a direct route of 20 miles through the wilderness. He decided on the latter course and in twenty days covered the distance, which was excellent progress in the conditions which nature and the patriot army put in his way. Trees were felled across his path, rivers diverted, stones rolled into the tracks, and bridges destroyed. Yet Fort Edward was reached on 30 July, three-quarters of the distance to Albany covered, and the navigable Hudson now available. The casualties he had suffered were minimal and the enemy had everywhere been worsted. Prospects seemed most encouraging.

Factors arose which made future success less certain. Although the Americans under General Schuyler had fallen back to the mouth of the Mohawk and their spirits were not of the best, yet they daily gained strength in numbers. Congress had sent Gates north to assume command and he was joined by Arnold and Benjamin Lincoln. Patriots in New England were thoroughly alarmed and volunteered to defend their property. Burgoyne's force was less able to cope. First, troops had had to be detached from Canada to occupy Ticonderoga and other posts, and the Indians were unreliable and drunken (whereas regulars were allowed only ⅜ of a pint of rum daily, drink was given to Indians 'without any Rule or Ration'). Secondly, supplies were a problem. Communications were lengthy and Schuyler had driven off the cattle and had taken grain from the area of British advance. If food was needed so were horses – 250 German dragoons had come on foot in the belief that they could catch new mounts along the Hudson shore. Thirdly, Burgoyne was isolated. By the time he left Ford Edward, on 13 September, he knew of the fate of St Leger's expedition and was aware that there would be no help at Albany from Howe, who had embarked for Philadelphia. Very few loyalists rallied to him and he was given misleading information on the strength of patriot feeling in the area.

The Bennington expedition in mid-August illustrated his difficulty. He learned that 30 miles south-east of Fort Edward there was an American depot with horses and general supplies. Colonel Baum, a non-English-speaking German, was sent with 800 men, including the unmounted dragoons, to seize equipment.Unknown to Burgoyne a fresh detachment of 1,500 New Hampshire militia had just reached Bennington, making a total force of 2,000 men. The ill-assorted British force was crushed; tories and Indians were useless, the Germans ran out of ammunition and reinforcements arrived too late; 900 men were lost and no supplies taken.

Burgoyne now had to take a crucial decision – whether to go on to Albany, despite difficulties, or withdraw to Ticonderoga. He was not a man to withdraw and, as he had criticized Howe's refusal to take risks, we should recognize the boldness of Burgoyne's decision. But this was a miscalculation, made for reasons of personal vanity and an unwillingness to accept criticism which would greet a withdrawal. Later he tried to shift responsibility for his decision to advance on to his orders, interpreting them to mean that he had no choice but to advance on Albany, an entirely fallacious reading.

On 13 September the British army, now 6,000 strong, advanced along the west bank of the Hudson. On 18 September they reached a point south of Saratoga, three miles from the strongly fortified American position on Bemis Heights. Patriots now numbered about 9,000 and Burgoyne was denied intelligence reports about their deployment or numerical strength. The British advance was blind, through thick woods, and at the first battle of Freeman's Farm, Burgoyne's three columns lost contact with each other which made reinforcement difficult. A bloody battle followed; Morgan and his Americans could not break the British line and were forced to retreat, losing control of the Farm, but preventing any major attack on Gates's position on the Heights. British casualties were over 600 irreplaceable men; each day brought new recruits for Gates.

There was then a lull in the fighting. Clinton in New York had sent word that he would lead 3,000 men up the Hudson not so much to get Burgoyne out of trouble, but to relieve pressure. Even in mid-September Clinton did not realize Burgoyne's difficulties because no news had been sent. Only on 5 October when the expedition was under way did Burgoyne's position become known to him. Clinton could not hope to extract Burgoyne from the Saratoga trap; his resources were too limited and time was pressing. Burgoyne also tried to shift responsibility for future decisions onto Clinton, a shoddy piece of evasion to which the reply snarled back, 'Sir Henry Clinton cannot presume to send orders to General Burgoyne'.

Clinton made a wholehearted effort to get to Albany. By swift, decisive movements he cleared the lower Hudson of enemy forts and booms. His transports came within 45 miles of Albany by

mid-October. But on 18 October with the possibility of the lower
Hudson remaining a British sphere of influence and Burgoyne's
defeat partially offset, Clinton was ordered to withdraw and reinforce Howe at Philadelphia. He had no option but to obey.

To return to Burgoyne – a second battle took place at Freeman's Farm on 7 October. A British flanking movement failed
and the Americans launched a frontal assault. By nightfall the
line had held, but at the cost of 700 casualties. Burgoyne therefore ordered a retreat to the north, to open ground around Saratoga where Gates, refusing to commit himself to open battle,
surrounded the dispirited British force and maintained a ceaseless bombardment.

Surrender was agreed: negotiations opened on 14 October.
Gates at first required an unconditional surrender but Burgoyne
asked for a 'convention' whereby the British army would lay
down its arms, sail back to England and not serve in America
again during the war. Gates knew that Clinton was moving up the
Hudson and, afraid of delay, agreed to these terms. Thus on 17
October the army at Saratoga laid down its arms. The convention
was never kept. Congress did not wish to break the terms made
by its general, but excuses were found to prevent the embarkation
of the troops. They were held in Virginia and their numbers
dwindled to 1,500 by 1782. Burgoyne was luckier. He was
allowed to return to London on parole where he produced a full
and moving apology for his action, blaming everyone except himself. The debate revolved around Germain and Howe and since
all were members of Parliament they had the freedom of the
House in which to vent their spleen. No good came of this to
anybody.

Howe had succeeded in the occupation of Philadelphia but elsewhere the British record for 1777 was grim. Undoubtedly the one
decisive engagement so far had been Saratoga which brought a
reappraisal of manpower, aims and methods. There was a clean
sweep of British commanders in the field; Burgoyne was barred
from further participation under the terms of the convention;
Carleton had been so insulted by Germain that he resigned command in Canada to General Haldimond; of greater significance
was the resignation of General Howe. His lack of imagination had
been primarily responsible for the absence of success; the structure of war, its strategy and administration, had proved too much
for him to handle. Sir Henry Clinton, therefore, replaced him as
commander-in-chief.

News of Saratoga reached London in December and was immediately debated in the House of Commons. The Opposition
leapt at Germain's throat and the Cabinet was divided. It was at
this point that Lord North became deeply pessimistic about the
outcome of the war and was quite prepared to resign. A possible
successor was the Earl of Chatham, but his death in April 1778
prevented any transfer of power, and as usual the Opposition
was hopelessly divided over a positive course of action. Germain
recognized that a land war required numbers of troops beyond
his resources, so the Cabinet turned to a sea-based strategy.

Congress, which had left Philadelphia for York, Pennsylvania,
received news of Saratoga with bells and cannon. The surrender
of the British troops made the permanent subjection of America
impossible. Much of the despondency which had characterized
the American war effort lifted and hopes of victory were commonly shared. Yet Saratoga did not help to strengthen Washington's position. Until October 1777 he had been a singularly un-
successful commander and a movement began to displace him in
favour of Gates, popular hero of the day. The so called 'Conway
Cabal' was never able to outwit the commander-in-chief who
used written evidence which came his way to cast confusion

among his enemies both in Congress and the army. The winter of 1777–8 was uncomfortable for them all – for troops at Valley Forge, and for those responsible for the conduct of the war. A lack of unity characterized the patriot administration.

Saratoga had made impossible the efforts of the Peace Commissioners. In 1776 the admiral, Lord Howe, and his brother, the general, had been given powers to accept the submission of American rebels and to consider the restoration of legal government. They lacked powers of negotiation, and could offer no concessions. Use of their authority was first made in July 1776 when General Howe landed on Staten Island. A Proclamation of Pardon was issued and a letter was sent to Washington proposing discussions, an offer which was rightly rejected. Even after the capture of New York Congress was not impressed by the Commission and not until the campaign in New Jersey did the pardons have conspicuous success, when the whole state seemed to flock to the royal banner. This proved illusory when British troops withdrew. So ineffectual was the Commission that Congress actually published its initial proclamation so that Americans could know how little they might expect from the king.

Yet the most important effect of Saratoga was in Europe. France was now persuaded to enter the war openly. This meant that the Revolution was no longer a Civil War but a world-wide struggle between the two major European powers.

PART V
American Victory in a European War

[25] EUROPEAN INVOLVEMENT

On receipt of the news from Saratoga the French government saw the opportunity to enter an advantageous war. From a position of tactful neutrality laced with surreptitious aid to the rebels, France was prepared to commit herself fully against Britain. So was Spain, hoping to gain from an alliance with France rather than with the United States. In this way the War of Independence exploded into a major European conflict. The prelude to this struggle, however, was a period of diplomatic and economic intrigue.

American foreign policy in the opening days was concerned more with commercial than diplomatic objectives. In April 1776 Congress opened American ports to the free trade of the world, attracting as a consequence gun runners, smart alecs and riff raff to supplement genuine traders. It was as a merchant that Silas Deane appeared in Paris in July 1776 with orders to obtain supplies and loans on as favourable terms as possible. Arthur Lee had already contacted a French political agent in London to arrange the initial cargo of munitions. Subsidies were forthcoming from the French and Spanish governments and the fictitious company of 'Roderigue Hortalez' was established. Thus for two years the French actively assisted the Americans with money, equipment – Saratoga would not have been won without

French guns – and the hospitality of their ports. Privateers, especially in the West Indies, could put into French ports with comparative impunity.

On the Declaration of Independence the international situation was clarified. No longer was it a domestic quarrel, but a war for freedom waged by a sovereign power. Franklin was sent as Commissioner to France to woo support for the new nation and the recognition of independence. He was a model ambassador, both shrewd and personally popular. In 1777 scores of Frenchmen enlisted in the patriot army, many of them seeking high rank and equivalent pay, causing considerable difficulties for Washington. But the volunteers did include a legendary hero of the Revolution, Lafayette, and a Prussian drill master, Steuben, whose contribution was immense. Saratoga strengthened Franklin's hand, but the initiative in all diplomatic affairs lay with France.

Since 1763 France had hoped to attack British supremacy through her colonies. The importance of sea power was recognized, a fleet was built, and adequate stores and ammunition prepared. Louis XVI, who came to the throne in 1774, appointed the Comte de Vergennes as his Minister of Foreign Affairs, a post he held throughout the American war. He continued his predecessor's policy of maintaining the fleet, but at first did not consider that the events of 1774 indicated a new situation. In 1775 he sent observers to London and to America; their reports convinced him of the wisdom of aid for the colonists in order to wound British interests as far as possible without recourse to war. In 1776 1 million livres worth of supplies was given; 2 million in 1777.

What was French policy in 1777? She had virtually abandoned any hope of a colonial empire, and was not interested in snatching the American colonies for herself once they were prised from the British. Her ambition was certainly to hold and strengthen her possessions in the West Indies, but essentially she was a European power interested in wealth as a necessity of European grandeur. She wanted to reverse the verdict of 1763, and was confident that any damage inflicted on English trade or power would automatically benefit France. Caution was advisable in these early stages lest the Earl of Chatham return to head a British war effort – Vergennes feared that he would make a swift peace with the Americans and then turn on the French West Indies and destroy her there. Vergennes therefore insisted on the trappings of friendship towards Britain – although the British were well informed through spies of the close relationship between France and the United States. Ideas of democracy did not appeal to the French court, nor particularly to the people, only to the 'philosophes' and their readers, but the colonial cause did create popular support if only because it defied the British. One factor militated against intervention – finance. The economy was precarious and Turgot, Minister of Finance, was opposed to a war which would destroy the progress made since 1774 towards stability. In the event, he was right.

Spain, whose king was also a Bourbon, had a more definite stake in America. Her colonies bordered the Mississippi and covered the whole of Central and Southern America, apart from Brazil, which belonged to Portugal. She was not partial to the ideal of independence, a contagious disease which could prove dangerous, but she was prepared to weaken British power which might, if not checked or divided, drive her out of the Americas all together. Relations with France were variable and coordination proved troublesome; to be effective the Bourbon powers needed to act in concert, but this was rarely achieved. Aid was given to the Americans – 1 million livres in 1776, for example – but independence was never recognized and Spain did not enter the European war until 1779.

France recognized the United States in December 1777, to forestall any peace moves which the British government might offer after Saratoga. A possible complication arose early in 1778 when Joseph II of Austria seized Bavaria, an action which led to war with Prussia. France was wooed by both parties, but she ignored even the possibility of success in the Netherlands for the opportunity to break the British at sea. Vergennes was determined not to fight on two fronts. In February 1778 he signed the treaties of Commerce and Alliance with the Americans. The terms were wholly favourable to the American cause: if there were war between France and Britain, then France and the United States were to remain firm allies until independence was assured; neither country would sign separate peace treaties without the consent of the other; France was to have no claim on the North American mainland east of the Mississippi; and she could have a free hand in the West Indies. In March Franklin was received officially for the first time at Versailles – the United States was now an accredited power and an ally of the greatest of European courts.

Spain attempted to make her neutrality pay by demanding Gibraltar, but to no avail. In June 1779 she was at war with Britain as an ally of France. She continued to give aid to America – $400,000 in subsidies and $250,000 in loans, and she added to the isolation of Britain. Yet in many ways her alliance was suspect. The French historian Doniol said, 'an alliance so sought for . . . had rarely been so useless, so barren of results, or a better justification to powers . . . who believe in putting little trust in allies'.

No invasion of England by a joint Franco-Spanish force ever looked feasible; cooperation between the fleets was minimal; Gibraltar diverted the attention of their fleets to no strategic advantage; Spanish conquests in Florida in 1780–1 did not divert the attention of a major British force; and from the outset the problem of the Mississippi threatened to anger the Americans. The Franco-Spanish alliance does, indeed, look abortive. The Spaniards worked diplomatically for their own advantage, refusing to recognize American independence and tending to weaken the ties between France and the United States.

But Britain was faced with additional foes as the war went on. Holland grew increasingly hostile, especially in defence of her doctrine that all trade carried in neutral ships was free from capture. Strangely the Dutch, the most powerful republican power in Europe, were not sympathetic towards the republican aspirations of the New World; there was greater encouragement from absolutist France. Holland was bound up with her own internal political troubles and consideration of trade. Late in 1780 the Dutch were labelled 'non grata' by the British government. They became open belligerents and Admiral Rodney captured and devastated the Dutch island of St Eustatius in the West Indies, depriving the Americans of a most valuable source of supplies.

The isolation of Britain was virtually completed by the agreement of many nations in the League of Armed Neutrality of 1780. Denmark, Sweden and Russia took the initiative and the League later included Prussia, Austria, Portugal and the Two Sicilies. The point at issue was the rights of neutrals with regard to the shipping of cargoes in time of war, and the right of Britain, in particular, to search and confiscate ships supplying the enemy. Whereas the British continued the traditional right to confiscate naval stores, the French offered a more generous principle of 'free ships, free goods'. The confusion lasted until 1780 when the three major Baltic powers not only laid down principles to protect their shipping, with armed assistance if needed, but also closed the Baltic to belligerent operations. French diplomacy had therefore triumphed, although Russia was not interested in full-blooded war against Britain, nor in acknowledging American independence.

The British situation was increasingly groggy. Even before Saratoga Lord North had been anxious to relinquish the leadership, afterwards he was desperate. He advocated Chatham's claim, but the king was adamant – Chatham would be acceptable only as a member of the ministry, never as its leader. With the probability of France entering the war the government sent emissaries to Paris to talk with Franklin, but this only hurried Vergennes into the February treaties, so that North realized by Spring 1778 that he was committed to a European war. Preparations had to be made for the opening shots.

Consequently there was a reappraisal of British policy. This was twofold – a new approach to the United States with a view to peace; and a shift of military and naval emphasis from the northern to the southern colonies on the mainland of North America, to the West Indies and to the Atlantic.

Peace with the ex-colonials was seen as a necessary preliminary to a successful war against France. Terms for the new commissioners were, therefore, a dramatic reversal of previous policy and looked like an admission of failure: taxation by Parliament was renounced; Congress was recognized as a fully legal body; Americans were given security of their charters, the right to raise troops, and the withdrawal of royal troops in time of peace. British rights were reduced to the regulation of trade, provision of a navy and the American honouring of debts plus restoration of loyalist estates. The vexed question of independence, upon which the Howe brothers had not been allowed to dwell, was not to be refused but referred back to London. The Earl of Carlisle led a three-man mission. He was disgusted to find on arrival in America that the new military strategy made his task virtually impossible. The evacuation of Philadelphia implied the over-throw of the British war machine; so, with the possibility of out-right victory, Americans were unwilling to listen to patronizing overtures from London. Congress refused to negotiate without recognition of independence and Carlisle returned home empty-handed in the autumn of 1778. Peace moves had failed again.

Of greater significance in 1778 was the action to meet war with France. Naval strength held the key to everything, and here there was much wanting. The Cabinet had been slow to supplement the fleet, but by late 1777 fears of French preparations had forced them to help Lord Sandwich supply 42 ships of the line in Europe, and eight abroad; this contrasted with the Bourbon fleet of France and Spain with its 42 ships at least in Europe, and 21 in American waters. Since it had lost its American seamen the British fleet was faced with a considerable problem of manpower. Recruitment was difficult, especially with the army competing for men, and with the high incidence of sickness. Fever and scurvy raged virtually unchecked. Crucial supplies were hard to come by also, especially timber for great masts. The usual American source of supply had been closed and later the Armed Neutrality prevented Stettin oak reaching the dockyards.

In 1778 the French navy called the tune. Vergennes's policy was to engage the attention of a British fleet in the Channel and then to detach a squadron to an overseas station and prove decisive there. He had an advantage in that his fleet, divided between Toulon and Brest, could slip into the Atlantic with comparative ease; a blockade was impossible. Britain was sensitive about the threat of invasion and was unwilling to weaken her Channel fleet, yet she needed to strengthen forces in the Mediterranean, West Indies and off the coast of America.

A new strategy was therefore devised to forestall French activity. If the French island of St Lucia in the West Indies could be captured, this would afford a fine harbour and divert attention from British islands which were garrisoned by only 1,800 troops in all! To lose the West Indies would seriously undermine the economy as it was then understood, and an opportunity to capture islands from the French was eagerly taken by the king at least. Clinton was therefore to evacuate Philadelphia, and Lord Howe with 5,000 troops and a sizable fleet was to attack St Lucia. Other troops would reinforce Florida, New York and Halifax. In June 1778 the Cabinet learned that the Toulon fleet under Estaing was in the Atlantic probably bound for America; this forced them to detach 13 ships under Admiral Byron – ominously nicknamed 'Foul Weather Jack' – from the home fleet for service off America.

In this way the American war became the concern of all major European powers. Britain was forced to deploy her forces thinly over land and sea, and problems of communication and administration were magnified tenfold. Only the king retained true optimism, although the war became more popular in 1778 when the traditional bogey of France was involved. In the House of Commons the Opposition remained as divided and ineffectual as ever.

[26] THE WAR IN AMERICA 1778–81

1778–9

General Howe had spent a splendid winter at Philadelphia. The beautiful Quaker city was the setting for a series of magnificent social occasions – parties, cock fights, balls and in early spring, horse racing. Some officers ruined themselves at the gambling tables and were forced to sell their commissions and return home; others were ruined in love; few were ruined in battle since only light skirmishes took place. Even with the advent of better weather Howe continued to sit tight until relieved by Clinton in May. A fantastic celebration was organized in honour of Sir William – the Mischianza. Beginning with a full regatta, there then followed a regal procession and medieval tournament, capped at night by a ball and firework display, reputedly the first gunpowder Howe had smelt in six months.

Sir Henry Clinton (1738–95) was to hold supreme command until the end of the campaign. A soldier of no mean ability, as his progress up the Hudson towards Burgoyne had shown, he was never convinced of his own prowess and often withdrew from facing the realities of any situation. Conscious of his dignity, he was very tetchy and quarrelled with his fellow officers. Probably the most serious quarrel was with Admiral Arbuthnot, commander of the fleet at New York, and the situation in 1781 was not helped by the deterioration in his relationship with Cornwallis. His biographer, William B. Willcox, sees him playing a crucial role in the American war – certainly this is the case, and it is possible to lament that lack of self-confidence which led to further stultification of British success. He often tendered his resignation and in 1780 Germain rebuked him:

In times like these every officer . . . is called upon to stand forth in the defence of his Sovereign, and of his country; and if a general declines the service . . . by whom is this country to be served in dangerous and critical situations?

Professor Willcox believes that he lacked the gift for spectacular failure and that his reputation has suffered as a consequence. Burgoyne and Cornwallis were captured, Gage lost Bunker Hill and Howe allowed Washington to escape from New York. Perhaps it is possible to be more sympathetic to Clinton in such company!

In May 1778 Clinton was ordered to evacuate Philadelphia and disperse his forces to the West Indies, Florida, Halifax and New York. Philadelphia was not a satisfactory point of dispersion because the fleet could not cope with the numbers involved. Therefore Clinton, with considerable skill, devised a withdrawal to New York and subsequent deployment from there. The navy took off supplies and 3,000 loyalist refugees from Philadelphia and the army marched into New Jersey on a 90-mile journey across country.

By contrast to British junketing, Washington had spent a grim winter at Valley Forge in appalling conditions. Scarcities led to disease and famine, as Lafayette reported:

The unfortunate soldiers were in want of everything; they had neither coats nor hats, nor shirts nor shoes; their feet and legs froze till they grew black, and it was often necessary to amputate them.

Supplies were difficult to transport through the snow, but too often the organization was inefficient. Speculation and profiteering diverted stores from their proper destination and Congress did not give sufficient attention to appointments or the organizational machine. One consequence of this frightful hardship was desertion; 3,000 went into Philadelphia to surrender; officers on leave did not return. Washington himself felt isolated while the so-called 'Conway Cabal' in Congress tried to deprive him of command. Yet those soldiers who stayed at Valley Forge were doggedly loyal and were the nucleus of a Continental Army which inspired the whole nation. Morale improved as spring approached and was assisted by the arrival of the Prussian officer, Baron Steuben, whose drill methods were immensely rewarding; he swore at one and all through his interpreter, knew his job thoroughly and showed an intense concern for the welfare of his men. A martinet he certainly was, but he made a rabble look like a disciplined army.

Washington survived that winter. News of the French alliance was known in early May. This strengthened determination to refuse all peace offers from the Carlisle commission unless independence was first conceded. It also brought volunteers to the army and a newly invigorated militia. When Clinton, therefore, set out for New York with his twelve-mile supply train he offered a ready target. Washington launched an attack on Cornwallis's rearguard at the battle of Monmouth Courthouse on 28 June; Charles Lee led 4,000 men against some 6,000 redcoats, but Clinton, leading the battle in person, gained the initiative and drove the patriots back. At night he quietly disengaged his troops and completed the withdrawal to New York with fine judgment.

In July the French fleet under Estaing appeared off New York; for eleven days Lord Howe, not yet joined by Byron, and the French eyed one another across the harbour bar. Shallow water worried Estaing and he moved off without giving battle. Howe anticipated that a joint land/sea operation would be launched against Rhode Island and he sailed north in time to surprise the landings which were being made near Newport. The French put out to sea, but a gale dispersed both fleets, so no decisive engagement was fought. Sullivan, in charge of land operations, feared that he would be caught by a full British fleet and so retreated. Estaing had failed to take advantage of his superior armament before the arrival of Byron. It was a lost opportunity.

During the winter of 1778–9 the northern theatre of war was comparatively tame. Local skirmishes and coastal raiding were the extent of activity. Washington's headquarters were in New Jersey and his men were in position along the Hudson, but the French fleet had sailed for the West Indies. Keen disappointment was felt that so little had been achieved in 1778. The advent of the French had been expected to bring total success, and some Americans were content to allow their allies to bear the burden of the fighting. Morale again dipped and Washington could only doggedly administer his resources and maintain the war wherever possible. Clinton in New York was happy with the stagnation in the North which allowed him to supply the southern expeditions.

At the end of 1778 Clinton sent an expedition to St Lucia (see pages 180–1), and to Georgia: 3,000 men landed near Savannah in December and were joined by a detachment from East Florida. Within a month they had recaptured Georgia for the king, and the governor who had been driven out to London was able to return and maintain royal control for three more years. The climate in the South allowed the campaign to progress even in the winter months. Congress sent General Lincoln to regain

control but in March 1779 he was soundly beaten at the battle of
Briar Creek, fifty miles north of Savannah. He was forced to
move back to the sea to reinforce Charleston which was threatened by a British column in May. Outnumbered, the British
withdrew and the heat of high summer gave pause to the fighting.

The situation in 1779 was unhappy; strategy, as decided by the
Cabinet in London and agreed to by local commanders, favoured
operations in the South to capitalize any loyalist feelings and
detach the colonies from Congress. At the same time raiding
parties along the coast in the North were to wreak havoc among
supplies and persuade the militia to remain in home districts,
denying their services to Washington's army. Each area was
also to be encouraged to return to the allegiance of the Crown.
This seemed to offer brighter prospects than the pursuit of an
elusive Continental Army, but it again overestimated the extent
of loyalist support – Americans were less inclined than ever to
support the king. In the course of these raids Portsmouth,
Virginia, was occupied from New York; and Clinton led a successful expedition up the Hudson. Yet small setbacks undermined
Clinton's morale and by the autumn of 1779, he abandoned the
raids in favour of a fullscale expedition again to Georgia.

Communications were hazardous, especially since control of
the seas was no longer a British monopoly. This was vividly
illustrated when Estaing reappeared off Savannah in August
1779. He had achieved some success in the West Indies and now
answered an appeal from the Governor of South Carolina to
capture the Georgian seaport. The city refused to surrender so a
siege was laid. This was too slow a method for the French admiral
who was under orders to return to Europe, so a frontal assault
was launched but beaten back. Estaing sailed away without any
success in his three encounters off the North American coast.
Indirectly his action helped, because Clinton withdrew from
Rhode Island to concentrate on New York, giving the patriots
a fine harbour. British emphasis was now placed again on
operations in the South.

Not that Washington had acted decisively in 1779; he was
hampered by the financial insecurity of the country, the apathy

which made recruitment difficult, and the absence of whole-hearted French cooperation on the mainland. Inflation debased the currency, so that handkerchiefs cost $100 and a suit of clothes $1,600. To add to the confusion the British circulated counterfeit notes. Washington expected a British evacuation of the North and planned an invasion of Canada, but when the British failed to move off the invasion was abandoned. By 1780 Washington was again in despair, plagued by inactivity and financial bickering in the army.

1780-1: The South

The British military cause was decisively lost as a result of this twenty-month campaign. Not that it was hopeless from the outset, nor was it less than successful in the majority of actions fought. Yet it could rarely pin down a patriot army in order to defeat it decisively nor could it persuade Americans to return to the mild care of John Bull. Instead British troops were eventually outwitted; their numbers dropped; they became exhausted and demoralized. They raced across four States, Georgia, North and South Carolina and Virginia only to confuse the pattern of war, and then found themselves in a position where temporary mastery of the sea and a well coordinated land attack gave the combined force of France and the United States unquestionable superiority. At Yorktown in October 1781 the French alliance worked for the first and only time on the field of battle. It was sufficient to gain American independence.

In February 1780 8,000 troops landed in South Carolina. Clinton had had a stormy passage – one dismasted transport drifted for eleven weeks only to arrive at St Ives, Cornwall. An orderly advance was made against Charleston whose defences were commanded by General Lincoln. Outgunned and outnumbered the Americans left their escape too late, and on 12 May over 5,000 men surrendered. This was equivalent to an American 'Saratoga' – but the effect was not at all the same. Replacements could be found from near at hand, although Lincoln's failure,

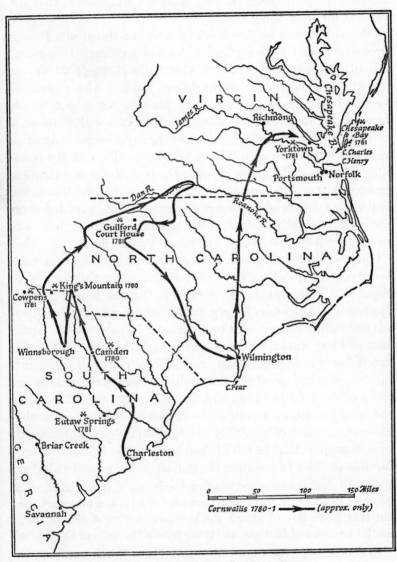

THE WAR 1776-83: *The Southern States*
(*adapted from Muir's Historical Atlas*)

the most dramatic since the loss of New York, showed that the war was far from being won.

Clinton returned to New York to meet the threat of a French force under the Comte de Rochambeau and entrusted command in South Carolina to Cornwallis. Cornwallis (1738–1805) was an adventurous soldier who emerged from the war with a personal record of courage and decisiveness. He won the respect of his men and his judgment was often overbold rather than timid, a refreshing fault among the generals of the day. Control in America was now divided between Clinton and Cornwallis with the possibility of misunderstanding between the two. Yet South Carolina seemed to be on the verge of total loyalty, so the situation in the South was fairly bright although the generals again trusted overmuch the strength of loyalist enthusiasm which at best was genuine, at least mercenary, but generally unreliable.

Congress declined to accept that the southern colonies were lost. Fresh troops under Horatio Gates, victor at Saratoga, were dispatched. His army met Cornwallis at Camden in mid-August. The result was a victory for regular British troops over Continentals and militia in a force twice its size. So decisive was the battle that, as Piers Mackesy says, 'Gates himself fled 200 miles on the fastest horse in the American army'. Despite everything, South Carolina was not pacified; Cornwallis hanged some militiamen who had deserted to the enemy, but this only brought reprisals and hardly endeared Americans to British sovereignty. So doubtful was Cornwallis of his ability to establish civil government with loyalist support that he felt obliged to carry the fight into North Carolina in order to maintain the initiative. He wrote to Clinton:

It may be doubted by some whether the invasion of North Carolina may be a prudent measure; but I am convinced it is a necessary one, and that if we do not attack the province, we must give up both South Carolina and Georgia, and retire within the walls of Charleston.

In September 1780 Cornwallis moved into North Carolina. He had barely entered the state when he learnt of the defeat of Major Ferguson at King's Mountain. A force of 1,000 men was destroyed, Cornwallis lost support at his rear and the patriots could acclaim a victory at long last to raise their spirits. The

British army, therefore, retired to Winnsborough, sixty miles south, where for three months it waited, harassed by the guerilla tactics of patriot raiders. By January 1781 fresh reserves arrived from Virginia, from Leslie's garrison at Norfolk which had been abandoned. Cornwallis, therefore mustered a force of 4,000 men and was encouraged to resume the advance when he learned that Benedict Arnold (for his defection to Britain see page 173) was leading an army into Virginia from the North.

On 7 January 1781 Cornwallis marched out of Winnsborough. General Nathanael Greene had replaced Gates as commander of the American army in the South. He is one of the underpraised heroes of the Revolution, a man of imagination who was not afraid to divide his limited forces when the occasion demanded, not afraid to retreat with skill in order to regroup. In support he had General Morgan and 'Light Horse Harry' Lee, the father of the great Civil War general, Robert E. Lee. By striking early at British communications, Greene forced Cornwallis to detach Colonel Banastre Tarleton to protect established posts. At the battle of Cowpens on 17 January Tarleton lost 800 men, 85 per cent of his command, in a resounding tactical defeat.

Cornwallis tried to pursue the victorious Americans but they slipped back across the flooded rivers of North Carolina into patriot territory without giving battle. Difficulties hampered British progress; sickness, desertion, casualties from snipers, lack of provisions and a weight of excess baggage all drained the resources of manpower and morale. By the time he reached the border of Virginia, Cornwallis knew he could not risk such a depleted army in the heart of enemy territory, so he withdrew. Greene's large, if raw, army waited at Guilford Court House and on 15 March Cornwallis, with an army only half the size of his opponent, seized the opportunity of an engagement. Despite every disadvantage Cornwallis and his men fought with tigerish enthusiasm, captured the enemy guns and won the day, but all at considerable cost. A quarter of the army was lost and victory could not be followed up. Greene was able to retreat, reform and strike down into South Carolina; Cornwallis withdrew to the coast at Wilmington.

An agonizing decision had to be made – should he go back 160 miles to Charleston to defend South Carolina, or march north 200 miles into Virginia to join Arnold? Communications between Clinton and Cornwallis were sketchy – for example Clinton had not been informed of the advance into North Carolina – and delay led to impatience. Mackesy believes that lack of coordination was due mainly to Clinton's failure to control his subordinate. Cornwallis, who believed Virginia to be the vital objective of the campaign in America, took the initiative by leaving Lord Rawdon with 8,000 troops scattered in South Carolina and Georgia, while he marched north again.

1780–1: The North

What had been Clinton's role before Cornwallis began his march into Virginia in April 1781? After the successful campaign at Charleston he returned to the 20,000-strong garrison at New York. Here he awaited both naval reinforcements under Graves, which brought Admiral Arbuthnot's fleet to 10 ships of the line, and the arrival of the French fleet under Ternay. The latter reached the coasts of Virginia in August 1780 and then proceeded north to Rhode Island, the harbour which Clinton had evacuated the previous autumn. Clinton hoped to launch a joint military and naval operation with Arbuthnot against Rhode Island, but so chronic were the lapses in communication between the two commanders that the opportunity passed. Not even the arrival of Admiral Rodney with 10 ships of the line – which gave overwhelming superiority against the French – led to the launching of an expedition. This was sheer neglect of an opportunity. All three men were culpable; so intense was their bickering and distrust that illfeeling paralysed the war machine.

By contrast, American hopes were raised by the arrival of the first official French army under the Comte de Rochambeau. Taking the advice of Lafayette, the French were prepared to be subject in all matters to Washington's supreme command. He planned an assault on New York but naval superiority was not achieved, so the project did not materialize. The immediate

effect of the French was to prevent the further dispersal of
Clinton's garrison from New York, but for some months the new
allies were unable to take a dynamic part in the war.

Yet the French presence was doubly valuable at the time when
Benedict Arnold conducted his treasonable correspondence with
the British. This brave soldier, who had nearly captured Quebec
in 1775 and who had forced St Leger to withdraw from the
Mohawk, as well as contributing to the campaign at Saratoga in
1777, had run foul of Pennsylvanian delegates in Congress. At a
court martial in January 1780 Arnold had been reprimanded for
comparatively trivial offences. This confirmed his intention to
change allegiance and he had been in contact with Clinton for
about eighteen months. His importance was enhanced by his
command of West Point, a fort strategically placed on the
Hudson. He agreed to turn this over to the British in September
1780, a move which would allow them an opportunity to cut
Washington's communications in two. Arnold met Major André
at a secret rendezvous to arrange details. Unfortunately André
was captured in no-man's-land by patriot militia, nicknamed
'Skinners' (the British gangs of irregulars were called 'Cowboys').
When searched, incriminating documents were found on him.
The game was up for Arnold. Taking advantage of the lull before
his complicity was known:

He ordered his horse to be saddled and his barge to be manned at
once. As he left the room he was followed by his wife, who had noticed
the agitation which had momentarily beset him. Arnold led her into
their chamber and there revealed to her the terrible truth. She scream-
ed and fell senseless at his feet. Arnold lifted her inanimate form on to
the bed, and, making his way downstairs galloped down a steep track
– still known as 'Arnold's path' – to where his barge awaited him.
Eighteen miles of water lay between him and H.M.S. *Vulture* . . . All
the way he sat in the bow of the boat with his pistols primed and within
reach – for he had made up his mind not to be taken alive.

So Colonel Whitton described the drama. Arnold travelled
safely and thereafter used his talents to defeat the patriots, although West Point was not to be British. Major André was
hanged as a spy, a harsh but technically correct sentence. It

served as a warning to others. Washington was badly shaken and by the end of 1780 he was critical of the nation's failure to support a standing army and of the absence of organization. He wrote:

The history of the war is a history of false hopes and temporary devices, instead of system and of economy.

We have no magazines nor money to form them, and in a little time we shall have no men if we had money to pay them. We have lived upon expedients till we can live no longer.

The northern war seemed a stalemate.

1781 saw Clinton prepared to support Cornwallis in the South with an expedition to Chesapeake Bay under Arnold. Leslie, who had left New York in October 1780 to take Norfolk, had joined Cornwallis. Arnold found no difficulty in occupying Portsmouth. Washington had been forced to put down a mutiny on New Year's Day and could ill afford troops until later in the month. He then sent Lafayette to assist Steuben in Virginia, but neither could dislodge the British force. In many aspects the patriot cause was desperate. The American army was likely to disintegrate and the French were increasingly aware of this weakness of their ally. Inflation threatened to destroy the economy. Stalemate seemed now to be to the British advantage. Certainly there was little cause for optimism among the Americans when Cornwallis marched to join Arnold on the shores of Chesapeake Bay in April.

Yorktown

Cornwallis joined with Arnold's force near Richmond, Virginia, in May 1781. He planned to develop an offensive but Clinton ordered him to move into Pennsylvania to attack stores, or else take up a defensive position, possibly at Yorktown. In this case Clinton originally wanted some troops to be withdrawn to New York to meet an expected Franco–American attack, but later allowed Cornwallis to keep his full complement. Clinton became defensively minded and through the summer was worried equally about the fate of New York and the exposed detachments in Virginia. In addition he wished to establish an anchorage for ships of the line in Chesapeake Bay, and it was as a result of this instruction that Cornwallis chose to fortify Yorktown. Although it held a commanding position to seaward, it was very exposed to a land attack.

The liaison between Washington and the French now showed itself to supreme advantage. An attack on New York was discarded, but Rochambeau made an appeal to Admiral de Grasse in the West Indies to bring his fleet and troops for a period to the mainland. De Grasse agreed to sail on 13 August for Chesapeake Bay and to stay until 13 October. On hearing this Washington gambled boldly. He left only 2,500 men on the lower Hudson and marched 7,000 French and American regulars to Virginia. The French fleet at Rhode Island set sail for Chesapeake Bay with siege equipment. Time was a vital factor. If the British fleet under Graves had realised what these movements signified, it could have occupied Chesapeake Bay before de Grasse arrived and the plan would have collapsed. This was not to be. De Grasse arrived with 28 ships of the line, 4,000 troops and some hard cash with which to help American finances.

Even so the British cause was not yet hopeless. Admiral Hood had arrived off New York from the West Indies in August with 14 ships of the line; he did not realize the extent of the crisis but was conscious of the necessity for speed. Graves and Hood sailed with 19 major ships, expecting to find perhaps the Rhode Island fleet off Chesapeake Bay. Instead on 5 September he found de Grasse with 24 ships to his 19, 1,800 guns against 1,400. There was no need for a French victory; an indecisive draw would enable the French to keep control of the seas and launch attacks on the Yorktown position.

The battle of Chesapeake Bay was an inglorious affair. At sunset when the fleets disengaged, the British were badly mauled, hampered by errors in signalling and inadequate coordination. For three days afterwards the fleets lay refitting within sight of each other. The French then retired within the mouth of the estuary between Cape Charles and Cape Henry where the Rhode Island fleet joined its fellows. Graves had thus lost every tactical advantage and withdrew to New York. A relief expedition was launched too late in October – the initiative at sea had been temporarily surrendered to a more numerous foe. De Grasse had cooperated with the Americans, joining the forces of the West Indies with those of the mainland in a way Germain had advocated for his own troops.

In Virginia, the French and the Americans massed 16,000 troops against 6,000; they held naval superiority; they possessed siege artillery. This was the decisive encounter of the American war but not the sort which Germain, North or the king had envisaged. The siege of Yorktown began on 28 September; the following day Cornwallis withdrew from his outer defences; on 9 October his earthworks were bombarded; he attempted to evacuate across the York river to Gloucester, but the weather was too stormy. Only 3,000 men remained for duty and artillery ammunition was expended. Cornwallis had no option. On 19 October his army marched out and laid down its arms, four years after Saratoga.

Who was responsible for the fiasco at Yorktown? Professor Willcox suggests that Cornwallis might have realized the seriousness of his position when the French fleet arrived. He could have retreated then, before Washington's army arrived. Possibly, he did not understand the nature of sea power at this juncture and immobilized himself. Yet Clinton also failed; he made no attempt to prevent Washington's march southwards, and allowed the French fleet to leave Rhode Island. Graves was not prepared to risk his fleet in making a dash for the mouth of Chesapeake Bay after the September battle was drawn. This move might have proved foolhardy. Far away, Admiral Rodney was also negligent. He returned to England from the West Indies believing that the French would send only a detachment to America. Hood, therefore, was allowed only 14 of the 20 ships of the line. The full quota would have given Graves numerical superiority.

More positive reasons included the strategy of de Grasse, whose promptitude and accuracy allowed a master plan to become operational; the boldness of Washington who gambled in withdrawing so many troops from the Hudson; and the help afforded by French troops under Rochambeau who fought so well under American command.

No further action of importance took place in the United States. Greene fought at Eutaw Springs; Rochambeau declined to launch an attack into Canada; Savannah was evacuated in 1782 but Charleston was held; and Clinton was occupied with loyalist troubles in New York until he was relieved by Guy Carleton in April 1782.

The effect of Yorktown was soon felt. News reached London in late November. Lord North burst out, 'Oh God! it is all over', a feeling shared generally in Parliament. The king was more optimistic and eyed the 30,000 troops who still remained in America. Many believed that only peace with the United States could prevent further disintegration. To understand this loss of morale it is necessary to realize that Britain was fighting not only a war on the mainland of America, but also a war at sea, in the West Indies and in India.

[27] THE WAR AT SEA

Home and Mediterranean Waters

Until France entered the war in 1778 British supremacy at sea had been easily maintained. The American navy consisted of privateers rather than squadrons, so pitched battles were impossible. This is not to underestimate the extent of damage to supplies and communications in the Atlantic or around British shores by heroes like John Paul Jones. Such activity could not, however, shake the supremacy of the Royal Navy. From 1778 sea power grew in importance. It proved vital at Yorktown and was responsible eventually for restoring some prestige to the Crown through the victory off the Saints in 1782.

The situation in 1778 has been outlined on page 163. Byron chased Estaing to America while Admiral Keppel commanded the Channel fleet with orders to prevent an invasion thrust, and to patrol in the eastern Atlantic. In mid-June the Channel fleet encountered two French frigates. Because the two countries were not formally at war, customary greetings would have had to be exchanged; instead, one of the Frenchmen delivered a broadside. The war had begun. In July the two fleets met west of Ushant and fought a drawn battle. Although the French withdrew under the cover of night, the British rigging was so shot away that their ships were almost immobilized. No decisive engagement materialized, despite efforts Keppel later made to find the French in the Bay of Biscay.

The New Year 1779 was celebrated by the court martial of Keppel on charges arising from accusations by his second-in-command, Admiral Palliser. Politics bedevilled the whole affair. Both men were members of Parliament but Keppel was a Rockingham whig and a supporter of the Opposition. Palliser was a friend of Lord Sandwich and the ministry. Palliser believed that Keppel was attaching to him the blame for the indecisive nature of the battle of Ushant. His counterattack was an error of judgment. The court martial was heavily biased in favour of Keppel, who was acquitted, and Palliser resigned. London was alive with violence and celebrated the acquittal without restraint.

Resignations in the navy grew to serious proportions when later the Admiralty ordered Keppel to strike his flag. The service was utterly divided, a disintegration equalled only in the army. Hardy, who had not been to sea for twenty years, became commander of the Channel fleet, and was faced with the entry of Spain into the war. In June a French fleet from Brest put out for Corunna to keep a rendezvous with the Spaniards. A joint force of 66 ships of the line planned to attack England and allow a force of 31,000 men to cross from Le Havre and St Malo to the Portsmouth area. Their timetable went seriously askew, however, and the fleet did not appear off Plymouth until mid-August. The hazards of invasion proved too numerous; not only had the fleet been at sea for a lengthy period and was sickly and ill-provisioned, but also the year was too far advanced. Decisive control of the sea had not been achieved, and the difficulty of establishing a beachhead in sufficient strength led to the withdrawal of the joint fleet in September.

Hardy had been caught off guard in the Channel. He stationed himself too far west and allowed the French to slip by. They believed that Hardy was further up Channel and did not take full advantage of the situation. By late August the Bourbons had lost their initial advantage. Hardy was back at Spithead and the enemy withdrew to Brest. The panic in England died down, although fierce criticism was levelled at the government for the apparent unreadiness of national defences.

In 1780 the ministry undertook a new strategy. An expedition to the West Indies was launched with a detachment to relieve Gibralter en route. The Rock was the key to control of the Mediterranean. It was not of supreme importance to Britain before the building of the Suez Canal nearly a century later, but since its capture in 1704 the public regarded it with immense affection. Its loss would have been a grievous blow to the prestige of any ministry. The Spaniards were not expecting a fullscale relief of Gibraltar. Rodney broke their fleet off Cape St Vincent, and brushed aside the blockading squadron to bring in supplies necessary for the survival of Gibraltar as a British fortress. He then proceeded to the West Indies, while the Channel detachment returned home.

Further relief expeditions were sent to Gibraltar in 1781 and 1782. Both were successful, but the 1781 expedition was bought at a high price. Reinforcements for America had to await its successful completion while de Grasse had already sailed for the West Indies. British failure to chase him was partially responsible for Yorktown. The third relief in October 1782 held immense political importance. Peace negotiations had begun in Paris and Spain hoped to gain Gibraltar, either by force or negotiation. Lord Howe's successful running of the blockade hastened everyone's determination to conclude a swift peace without undue attention to the Spanish claims. One Spanish success, however, was the capture of Minorca in 1782. The British garrison was beaten by scurvy as much as by the enemy, and only 800 fit men surrendered to 14,000.

Later Channel manoeuvres in 1780 and 1781 were not spectacular. British advantage lay in their new copper bottoms which prevented fouling, enabling ships to stay at sea longer and enjoy a faster turn of speed. Commanders of the fleet constantly changed, but with mixed success. Parker defeated the Dutch off Dogger Bank in 1781, but convoy protection was often inadequate. Several valuable convoys from the West Indies were lost, a terrible blow to trade confidence. By 1781 protection of the Jamaica convoy took precedence over interception even of the Brest fleet. Tasks allotted the Channel fleet far outstripped the resources available. Supplies and communications continued to be extremely vulnerable throughout the war.

Home waters remained one of the ministry's major preoccupations. Although an invasion was feared, the Bourbon fleets were fraught with as many difficulties as were the British. Limited resources allowed the French to use Brest virtually at will. No British blockade of the Mediterranean was feasible. Trade continued, but the Western approaches could never be guaranteed as safe.

The West Indies

The entry of France into the war brought the West Indies into prominence. All the islands belonged to one or other of the European powers whose merchants realized their wealth. In the House of Commons an influential lobby of merchant opinion protected trading interests, but most people realized the advantage of possessing these islands, if only for their sugar. If French or Spanish islands could be seized then this would be fine compensation for the loss of America; an even more optimistic view believed that the defeat of France in the West Indies would isolate America, which could then be subdued at pleasure. After 1778 both powers sought advantage in the fever ridden islands.

Clinton was ordered to dispatch an expedition to St Lucia in 1778. He withdrew from Philadelphia to New York before fulfilling his orders, and with the presence of Estaing off the coast it was well he did so. Reinforcement was essential since only 1,000 fit men guarded the islands; Grenada boasted 100, Jamaica 400. Yet such was the geography of the area that to strengthen each and every station was impossible. The ministry decided on a vigorous offensive to prevent piecemeal conquest. St Lucia, a French possession with a fine harbour and near the influential French island of Martinique, was selected.

Plans at first went awry. Admiral Barrington, despatched from England to command the Leeward Islands, waited all summer for the troops from New York. Meanwhile the French took Dominica and split the British Leeward possessions into two. When the English force did arrive Barrington took St Lucia in mid-December, only just before Estaing appeared with a 700-gun superiority. French assaults were beaten back. Estaing did not capitalize on his advantages before Byron arrived with the fleet from America in January 1779 to restore a parity between the two.

Ideally, the West Indies theatre of war should have been linked with movement on the mainland. Given the differences in climate it was theoretically possible for the army and navy to fight in the north during June to December, and in the West Indies from December to May. This assumed understanding and cooperation between commanders as well as favourable weather and communications. At no time did these materialize for the British. Too much petty bickering and unfortunate timing led only to the situation in 1781 when the Frenchman, de Grasse, showed how efficient the interchange system could be.

In 1779 General Grant's land force on St Lucia was reduced by a third within four months by death caused through sickness. Byron sailed north to protect a homeward bound convoy and in his absence St Vincent and Grenada were lost. On his return he mistakenly believed he still held naval superiority and in the ensuing battle was nearly destroyed. In these circumstances it proved impossible to send troops to help Clinton; men and ships were not available. In the autumn Estaing created havoc. He broke British communications between garrisons from the St Lawrence to the Gulf of Mexico, paralysing Clinton in New York and surprising the force at Savannah. Yet he could not break the defences there, and left for Europe in November.

The entry of Spain into the war in 1779 threatened both Jamaica and the Floridas. A British detachment on the Missis-

sippi surrendered in October, and two years later when Pensacola
fell, West Florida was lost.

Reinforcements from England were essential if the islands were
to be held. Admiral Rodney, therefore, sailed with 5,000 men for
the Leeward Islands and 3,000 men for Jamaica, a decision which
denied Clinton the troops he had asked for. George Rodney
(1719-92) was an embarrassing man; he was indiscreet in his
public and private life, especially in his financial dealings. To
escape his debtors he had fled to Paris in 1774 leaving his wife to
attempt a settlement of his affairs. Through a private loan he was
able to return from France before the outbreak of war in 1778,
but he was not asked to serve until a year later. Men still feared
that he would plunder the public purse to repay his debts.
Among his attributes were luck (he was never wounded), occasional boldness which was more spectacular than his many mistakes, and an ability to avoid arguments with the ministry. His
first success was the relief of Gibraltar in January 1780, from
whence he proceeded to the West Indies. In April 1780 Rodney
fought a drawn battle with the French off Martinique. Later in
the year he went north to New York (see page 172) where he suc-
cumbed to the prevailing acrimony, achieving nothing of note.

More positive activity in 1780 took place further west. General
Dalling in Jamaica had experienced difficulty in controlling the
island. Both the planters and the navy under Sir Peter Parker
found him intolerable. However, Dalling was ambitious and in
1779 had launched an attack on the Spanish Main, the narrow
strip of land joining North and South America. In 1780 he began
the main offensive on the San Juan river. Lake Nicaragua was
controlled but the advance could not continue because disease
had so ravaged the successful invaders. Although the ministry
had approved of this scheme, delighted with the prospect of a
base on the Pacific coast, troops originally designated for the
project were kept in Jamaica to aid vital defence there. The entry
of the Dutch into the war, together with the Armed Neutrality,
destroyed any further progress on the mainland, even if the
scheme had been feasible in the first place.

De Grasse dominated the events of 1781. British preoccupation with Gibraltar allowed him to leave Brest easily. He was not closely followed, so his destination was unknown. All too late the ministry sent reinforcements to America. The French fleet arrived in the West Indies and Tobago was seized in June, without Rodney giving battle. As a result de Grasse was able to accept the invitation from Rochambeau to assist in the Virginian campaign. Had Rodney with his numerical superiority engaged in a hard battle in midsummer, this might well have prevented de Grasse from volunteering his fleet. As it was, the French took 3,000 troops from San Domingo, money from Cuba and the whole fleet to Yorktown. It was brave and inspired.

Rodney did not expect de Grasse to take his entire fleet northwards; it was traditional for convoys to be escorted and ships returned to Europe for servicing. Assuming this, he divided his fleet. Some ships went to Jamaica; he himself, ill and tired, returned to England, and only 14 of the 20 ships of line available went to help Clinton. This was a major miscalculation which contributed to the failure at Yorktown.

After Yorktown the West Indies became the major battlefield. Only the capture of St Eustatius from the Dutch had redeemed the tale of failure in early 1781. The British situation now looked grim in all parts of the world. De Grasse, on his return to the West Indies, was in a position to continue the destruction of British holdings. Before Rodney returned to join Hood in February 1782 the French had captured St Kitts, Nevis, Montserrat and other islands in a grand sweep of success. Nor could Rodney prevent French reinforcement joining de Grasse for a full scale assault on Jamaica.

On 7 April 1782 de Grasse left Martinique for San Domingo and a rendezvous with the Spanish fleet. At first he tried to evade Rodney, who now had numerical superiority. He then tried to draw him away from the main convoy. Off the islands of the Saints, de Grasse gradually lost ships in the chase, but then came into action on 12 April; Rodney took advantage of his superiority and by the end of the day five French ships had struck their flag and de Grasse was a prisoner. The battle of the Saints was won.

Not that the enemy was broken. A joint French fleet could still be effective, but advantage now lay with the British as Jamaica was safe. There was a lucky element in British deployment in the West Indies in April 1782, but this was one of the few occasions in the war when fortune smiled on John Bull. It happened at a crucial moment. Peace negotiations were under way and the victory gave some dignity and bargaining power to British representatives in Paris. Victory at the Saints and Gibraltar in 1782, however, could not save Lord North's ministry.

India

British India was governed by the East India Company which had gained most benefit from the Peace of Paris in 1763. French political influence was minimal so it is hardly surprising that the American war was used as an opportunity to regain prestige in the East. This was even more likely when Holland, with her important possessions such as the Cape and Ceylon, became a belligerent. Not only did the Company fear external aggression but also it was aware of internal dissension. The Madras Presidency so antagonized local rulers that it provoked a coalition between the Nizam, Haider Ali and the Marathas. In 1780 the Carnatic was devastated by their army up to Madras itself, but Warren Hastings in Bengal sent reinforcements with partial success; yet in 1781 Sir Eyre Coote was almost starved into surrender when the French cut off his supplies from the sea. Hastings broke the triumvirate by detaching the Nizam and the Marathas from Haidar Ali who soldiered on with assurances of French support.

If internal trouble was a most difficult problem, French intervention was potentially disastrous. The Bailli de Suffren commanded a fleet which set sail in March 1781. If the French could break British naval supremacy in the Indian Ocean then the land forces would be as isolated as Cornwallis or Clinton in America. Haidar Ali could then destroy the power of the East India Company. To meet this threat troops were dispatched from England in 1782, men and ships which otherwise would have been used to defend the West Indies.

Initially, Suffren maintained a numerical superiority over the British fleet but could not destroy it. Three battles were fought before the 1782 reinforcements arrived; all were indecisive. By the spring of 1783 the French were also strengthened, and their attacks proved to be difficult to contain. It was with considerable relief that on 28 June news of the peace signed five months previously was received by British garrisons. At last the American war was really over. The empire had been saved.

[28] PEACE AT VERSAILLES 1783

British domestic politics since 1778 had been exceedingly troublesome for Lord North. Ireland, the colony on her doorstep, moved towards rebellion. Political power was at the discretion of the Anglicans, who numbered only ten per cent of the population. They owned five-sixths of the land, and from their ranks were drawn the very few men who controlled the Irish House of Commons. Economically Ireland depended upon her export of foodstuffs and linen, and the closure of American markets in 1776 was only partially offset by the opportunity to provision the army. Discontent took a novel form in 1778 when the possibility of a French invasion loomed large. Well-to-do Irishmen organized themselves into volunteer companies, obtained arms and uniforms and drilled with enthusiasm. Although prepared to repel the French they expressed open admiration for the aims of the American rebels. In particular they were conscious of the harsh treatment meted out to them by successive British governments, which contrasted with the leniency offered to Congress by the Peace Commissioners in 1778. Their cause prospered and by 1780 there were 40,000 volunteers under arms, 80,000 by 1782, and they were led by aristocrats and reformers of the Irish Parliament.

North allowed affairs to drift dangerously and not until 1780 did he relax controls on the export of a few articles like wool, and grant the Irish free trade with some of the colonies. This sop was accepted by the Irish Parliament, but there was no doubt that continued threats of force would alone win further concessions. Two great reformers, Henry Grattan and Henry Flood, led demands for an independent parliament and this was granted by the Rockingham administration in 1782 in the face of the York-town collapse. Truly the Americans had won for the Irish a greater measure of freedom than ever before, although the gift was soon to be lost.

In England the cry for parliamentary reform was heard again. The Rev. Christopher Wyvill and Sir George Savile M.P. led the Yorkshire Association which complained that not only was the incident of taxation exorbitant, but that excessive power was wielded by the ministry as a result of corruption. John Dunning indirectly attacked the power of the king by his motion in 1780 that 'the influence of the Crown has increased, is increasing, and ought to be diminished'. This was passed, a sure sign of North's failing grasp. Yet by September North had dissolved Parliament and emerged at the General Election only five or six votes weaker than before. His success was due in no small measure to the Gordon riots of June. A protestant mob in London threatened the security of propertied men. Opposition seemed to have gone too far and the foundations of social order were in jeopardy. The rush to restore established forms was swift. News from America and Ireland was also more pleasing, so North was given a renewed opportunity to achieve success in the world wide war.

His failure was epitomized in the defeat at Yorktown. Britain was isolated in Europe, her armies were humiliated in America. Support given to a Parliamentary motion, 'that all further at-tempts to reduce the revolted colonies to obedience are contrary to the true interests of this kingdom, as tending to weaken its efforts against its ancient and powerful enemies' demonstrated that North had failed to complete his stated objectives. Germain left the ministry in January 1782, a scapegoat for failure. Sand-wich also came under attack for the inability of the navy to engage the Bourbon fleets successfully.

In March, North was out of office. He had held the highest

place in the ministry for twelve years, most unwillingly and un-
successfully as war minister. The Cabinet under his direction
lacked the coordination and insight which a horrific international
situation demanded. They lost America and nearly lost an empire.
A collection of second-rate men left a legacy which could only be
salvaged through peace with America and concentration on
France.

The new ministry was led by Rockingham and Shelburne.
Their first move was to grant independence to the Irish parliament to prevent the emergence of another 'America'. General
peace was not so easily established. Until the death of Rockingham in July, responsibility for negotiations lay with Fox (dealing
with France and Spain) and Shelburne (responsible for America).
Their representatives in Paris were often at cross purposes as a
result of the struggle for power in London, a situation only of
value to the enemy. After Fox left the ministry Shelburne was
able to take a more positive line to wean the Americans away
from the French.

Negotiations for a peace settlement took many months. The
Americans could not afford to trust either of the major powers
implicitly. As early as June 1781 an American commission of five
men had been appointed to act with the advice, and under the
direction, of French ministers on all matters except independence.
In the face of strong opposition, Congress often reaffirmed its
intention to negotiate 'in confidence and in concert with his Most
Christian Majesty'. Apart from independence, the major issues
of any settlement were: Canada; Florida; control of, or access to,
the Mississippi; fishing rights; trade; debts; and loyalists.

After Yorktown independence could not be long denied. As a
result of their defeat off the Saints, the French were less strongly
placed. The British hoped to divide the allies by suggesting that
France was prolonging a war which was no longer in American
interests. A solution was complicated by the Spaniards who were
anxious to regain Gibraltar. The relief of the Rock in 1782 meant
she could not take it by force, and in the end neither Britain nor
France were prepared to bargain for alternative possessions.
Gibraltar remained British.

Vergennes wished to prevent disagreements arising between himself and the Americans. Ben Franklin, John Jay and John Adams were the commissioners most closely involved in peace arrangements. Franklin placed greater confidence in Vergennes than did Jay, who suspected that the European powers would be prepared to barter American interests for their own. This was possible since two sets of negotiations were proceeding simultaneously, between Britain and America, and Britain and the European powers. Both the Americans and the French, however, agreed that treaties would only be signed if terms were agreeable to them both. Jay in particular distrusted Spain, who refused to acknowledge American independence until Britain did so, and who expected the Americans to leave the Mississippi south of the Ohio river under Spanish control. In August he also learned that the French were prepared to jettison American claims to fishing rights and the western lands.

In the face of these threats to American sovereignty Jay dropped his previous insistence that Britain recognize full American independence before further negotiation. Instead, he accepted the British resolution to treat 'with the Commissioners appointed by the Colonies, under the title of Thirteen United States' – a strange mishmash of words, but sufficient to speed on the talks to an early conclusion.

Preliminary articles of peace were agreed on 30 November 1782 and were the same as the definitive treaties signed in January and September 1783. The Canadian boundary was not that of the Quebec Act, which had reached as far south as the Ohio River, but was on a line closer to the present-day boundary between the Atlantic and the Great Lakes, thus giving the Americans access to the western lands. The Mississippi 'from its source to the Ocean' was to be free and open to British and American subjects, an article designed to hold back Spain. A secret article which recognized British occupation of West Florida did not become operative since the treaty between the European powers ceded it to Spain. This was fortunate for the United States. The Spaniards proved weak neighbours; Britain would have proved a serious barrier to expansion into the south-west.

Americans were allowed the right to fish on the high seas and the liberty to fish the inshore waters of British North America, especially Newfoundland. All debts contracted before 1775 would be paid by 'creditors on either side'. Congress recommended to the legislatures of the States that the confiscated property of loyalists be returned, a weak article which virtually abandoned the loyalists to penury. They were allowed their personal freedom and the right to emigrate and eventually Britain paid nearly $20 million in claims. Finally, British troops were to be evacuated 'with all convenient speed', which led to later trouble around the Great Lakes.

These articles were signed by both British and American negotiators and a copy sent to the French court. The terms arranged were not to be operative until the Anglo–French treaty was completed, but Vergennes was annoyed that the signatures had been added without French consultation. It seemed that Congressional orders had been ignored. Franklin's tact smoothed over this possible eleventh hour rift between the allies. He explained that no slight had been intended, no attempt at deception made. His reasons were accepted, and on the strength of this he negotiated the last French loan, money vital to the solvency of the new nation.

France was hardly satisfied with the terms she obtained from Britain in January 1783. In the West Indies she gained only Tobago, handing back the other islands which she had captured. Further north she gained fishing rights off the coast of Newfoundland and kept occupation of her islands in the Gulf of the St Lawrence. In Africa she gained Senegal with its gum trade, but her biggest disappointment was her failure to recapture power in India. In no way did she return to the position of 1756; instead the situation of 1777 was restored, with her trading rights guaranteed. She did not even have the consolation of nurturing a grateful or subservient nation. The Americans were already too independent. Even the Spaniards, with their occupation of Minorca and Florida, seemed to gain more than the French. Only the Dutch, who failed to gain recognition for the principles of the Armed Neutrality and were forced to allow the British access to trade in the East Indies, seemed equally badly off. To offset minor gains, however, the French were burdened by an additional financial liability. Necker had raised funds by loans rather than taxation, so the Treasury was saddled with new capital and interest charges. This was the most important legacy of the war.

How had Britain fared? Her greatest loss was the American colonies. Shelburne hoped to maintain an alliance with the United States, even to the extent that London would still determine her foreign policy. Even more he wished to strengthen commercial ties on the free trade principles of Adam Smith. He was accused of a total surrender to Britain's enemies and in February 1783, although the peace was grudgingly approved, he resigned. Considering the weight of opposition against her, Britain emerged from the war more creditably than might have been considered possible. She kept Canada, the West Indies, India and command of the seas – her major possessions. It was a decent withdrawal. In 1781 she could have lost her empire; in 1783 she was allowed to keep her supremacy in all areas, save the United States.

In Congress stormy debates had been held over the propriety of the action of the Peace Commissioners. Many felt that they had played into the hands of the British and had been unjust to their French allies. But no decisions were taken and general delight was felt when the January treaty was known on 23 March 1783. Congress was engaged at the time in one of the periodic disputes with the army over pay, so peace news was welcome to strengthen the credit of the government. The Newburgh addresses advised the army to seize its own justice, but Congress kept control and disbanded the army with promise of payment. Peace had returned to America.

It may be said that the War of Independence was not so much won by the Americans as lost by the British. This would be to deny the effectiveness of the American contribution to victory. Examples of individual heroism, and victory on the field of battle, in particular by a tenacious Continental Army, cannot be overlooked. Nor should the organization afforded by Congress be underestimated; it provided an inadequate but continuing control over colonial affairs. But all too often the British effort was ineffective and her advantage not pressed home, for reasons which by now are familiar. Crucial to the outcome of the war was French intervention. This both stiffened American resistance and weakened, through dispersal, the British effort. Without the assistance of supplies, navy and manpower from France, it is probable that Britain would have won the military victory in America. This does not mean that she could have subdued the colonies indefinitely, but the combined Franco-American victory at Yorktown makes such speculation meaningless.

PART VI
The Aftermath of War

[29] CONDITIONS IN THE UNITED STATES DURING AND AFTER THE WAR

Not until the twentieth century has war touched the bulk of any civilian population directly. True, the economic and social effect of war was generally transmitted, but butchery was localized in a way which aerial bombardment has now made impossible. By old world standards the American war was a civilized affair. The number of men killed was small – by February 1778 the total British dead in action was no more than 1,200 – and the conduct of the armies was usually restrained. This was due partly to the limited size of the armies taking the field, partly to the British policy of restoration of civil government rather than its destruction, and partly to the wide expanse of territory over which the battle roamed. There were no trench battlefields and war rarely passed by twice. Armies lived off the land, but more was bought than stolen. Garrison posts were few and far between, often ill-manned, so British troops could in no way control the civilian population.

Only in the South and on the frontier did the war take an increasingly malicious aspect. Indian raids, family feuds, robbery and confusion in a lawless land led to acts of terrorism committed in the name of either side. The epileptic brother of the tory, Major 'Bloody Bill' Cunningham, was whipped to death, and his father beaten by a whig, Captain Ritchie, in South Carolina. Cunningham walked some 150 miles to slay Ritchie. Such a vendetta was not infrequent,

Hardship during the war was felt by many. Fishermen could not operate for the naval blockade; those on fixed incomes, especially salaries, suffered from galloping inflation. Poorer workers in the towns who could not provide their own food were victims of the vicious price rise. The officers and men of the Continental Army complained justifiably of the financial burden they and their families were expected to bear. Only the quarter-masters who could rig contracts with merchants were comfortably provided for. Congress itself experienced financial embarrassment but hardly treated the army with the respect it deserved. Dissatisfaction came to a head in 1783 when the Newburgh addresses threatened mutiny at the time of peace. Congress turned this threat by promising full pay for five years as a bounty for the officers, and three months' pay for the men. By June 1783 the army dispersed with the promise of payment and disappeared as a political force in war or peace. Paper money aggravated the problem of inflation, especially when individual States refused to cooperate with Congress in any form of control.

Farmers, merchants and financiers made profits. Although transportation caused difficulty, the provisioning of both armies and the cities created an enormous demand for foodstuffs. Since ninety per cent of the population were farmers, the majority was shielded from the worst ravages of inflation. The merchants, although a small group, became most influential in political circles and grew rich from the proceeds of war. They had freedom to raise prices to levels which they chose, given the shortage of goods and lack of competition. In Boston in 1777 the merchants refused to sell supplies of coffee and sugar, because they were waiting for prices to rise. Profit margins were unreasonably large, so much so that merchants were distrusted in some areas. In Maryland the assembly resolved that no merchant could represent it in Congress, since it was alleged that Samuel Chase had used Congressional information to corner the wheat market. There was no control of prices, no worthwhile taxation. Many merchants extolled the virtues of monopoly and profit making. The naval blockade off the coast was never sufficiently tight to discourage privateering or the European trade, and so losses were worth bearing with profits so attractive. Revolutionary trade confirmed the status of men like Hancock of Boston.

Financiers were also well off. The founding of the Bank of North America in 1781 by Robert Morris was a new departure. Morris engaged in private and public business simultaneously. For a period in 1782 he was virtually dictator of the United States as the superintendent of finance and founder of the Bank. Public credit depended upon his manipulation of funds, but it appears that he used his powers to favour his friends and enrich himself, or so the charges ran. True or false, he resigned in 1784. The bank was blamed for many of the financial hardships of the times and its charter was revoked by Pennsylvania in 1785. Nonetheless it continued in business, and inspired the foundation of similar banks in Boston and New York. All came under fire when times were bad, but they all contributed to the sophistication of business.

The one group helpless in the course of war was the tories. They bore the brunt of patriot hatred and at the same time were largely ignored by British commanders in the field. Some of the most influential tories, like William Byrd of Westover, Virginia, stayed at home unmolested; others were so insignificant as to be not worth noticing. But the majority automatically lost all civil rights, even the right to work in some States, and their property was confiscated to pay for the war effort. Jonathan Sewell wrote:

Everything I see is laughable, cursable and damnable; my pew in the church is converted into a pork tub; my house into a den of rebels, thieves and lice; my farm in the possession of the very worst of all God's creation.

During the war they were often banished from their States with or without trial. Many left Boston with Howe in 1777, or Philadelphia with Clinton in 1778. Some of the more wealthy came to London but shortage of funds as well as lack of status closed the heights of society to them. Within the United States only New York remained a centre of loyalist feelings. After Yorktown the city experienced a desperate orgy of Anglophilia; a band played 'God Save the King' every hour, and a magnificent firework display exploded on the king's birthday, but the festivities were soon over. Most tories believed that they had been thanklessly abandoned by the British during negotiations for peace. No security or redress was forthcoming in the terms, except by grace and favour of the individual States.

The patriots were far from generous to the tories. After all, they argued, the tories had helped British armies in the field and had gambled on British success. Had this materialized then the fruits of victory would have been sweet indeed. States did not look kindly on tory claims for the return of confiscated property, nor were they socially acceptable. The vehemence of their rejection took them generally by surprise. Permanent exile, therefore, became normal. Some remained in England, disgruntled about their fate and comparing it unfavourably with life in America. Many from the southern States in particular went to the West Indies. A projected Royalist settlement in Australia did not materialize. The bulk of the refugees went north into Canada – to Nova Scotia, New Brunswick and Ontario.

The number of exiles was in the region of 80,000, a noteworthy exodus. Professor Palmer suggests that there were twenty-four exiles per 1,000 of the population in the American Revolution, whereas in the French Revolution there were only five per thousand. These figures are significant. First, it shows the extent of the upheaval caused by the war. The United States lost not only her dead but the exiles. These were old settlers who had been responsible for creating American strength. Immigration fortunately soon made good this numerical loss.

Secondly, the exiles were often the 'aristocracy' whose disappearance weakened the force of tradition in American life. Their ideology could have had a profound effect on future thought, and in rejecting a tory philosophy Americans were the poorer. They cut themselves off from a source of European civilization and, by ignoring the tory interpretation of the revolution and the nature of society, the United States went another step forward to the horror of uniformity.

Thirdly, the exodus to the north was sufficiently numerous to achieve the end for which the British government had striven for twenty years; namely, the colonization of Canada by Anglo-Saxon Protestants. The climate was rougher, the exiles were often homesick, nor did they mix with the French, but they were prepared to pioneer as their ancestors had before them.

However, the American war did not achieve a social revolution. It remained essentially a political change. Many of the outstanding social figures of pre-war days were patriots and reaped the fruits of victory. Their status was magnified rather than diminished. Although the confiscation of Crown and tory estates led to a wider ownership of land, yet many of the lots available were purchased by those already wealthy or those who were speculating. A disappointing percentage seems to have come to the yeoman smallholder. In New York, for example, Roger Morris's estate was divided among 250 people, but other estates went to the Livingstons and Roosevelts, the patricians of the day. The Penn family was allowed to keep 500,000 acres in Pennsylvania, and the tory Lord Fairfax maintained his estates in Virginia – hardly the destruction of the wealthy. Even the disappearance of old English forms such as quitrents, primogeniture and entail was not as significant as might have been expected, and even served to help the rich rather than the poor. Before 1776 quitrents had been generally evaded, and in Virginia primogeniture had been enforced only when an owner died without a will. Landholding remained important since most voting rights were conditional on land or property qualifications.

The Churches lost some of their privileges in the upheaval. The Anglican church was particularly vulnerable. It was forced to give up the Royal Supremacy and separated from the Church of England; it also lost its privileged establishment in the South and New York. In Virginia, Jefferson fought a lengthy battle to assert the principles of full religious liberty. Not until 1786 did he carry a declaration of religious equality, which asserted the right of any man to hold public office irrespective of religious belief, even if he were an atheist. Only in New England did the churches maintain their hold. The Congregationalists held fast their domination until the nineteenth century, Massachusetts finally abandoning the cause in 1833.

Slavery remained a problem in the field of human liberty. The carrying trade across the Atlantic was prohibited by the majority of States during or after the war. The Constitution of 1787 recognized the institution of slavery when it calculated slaves as 'three-fifths of other persons' in assessments of the population in States for the purpose of representation in the House of Representatives. Slaves were to be extradited, and the final prohibition of the external slave trade was delayed until 1808. Difficulties in enforcing this law meant that its evasion was frequent. In the North the war was a spur towards abolition. Vermont proclaimed it in 1777, Massachusetts in 1780, New York in 1799 among others. In the South the invention of the cotton gin by Eli Whitney in 1793 placed slavery in a different light. Although many slave owners had accepted that the Declaration of Independence implied the eventual manumission of slaves, economic considerations now made the slave indispensable. Thus the hopes raised by the war failed to materialize. General indifference was common in both North and South for the lot of the slave. The first anti-slavery society was founded by Quakers in 1775 but enthusiasm for its principles was not apparent for over fifty years.

In essence, the effect of the revolution was to confirm the social structure of the States. Change would in future be modifications of the forms rather than their replacement. In this sense America has been less radical than Britain. Yet historians have not examined the full field of social and political forces in the post-war period, and no definite thesis has emerged. Perhaps it is unreasonable to expect one.

Immediately following the war there was a spending spree. All the luxuries long since denied flooded into the States. But shortage of money led to falling prices and, despite the extension of credit, the drying up of trade in many areas. Lord Shelburne in 1783 had hoped to maintain the close trade connections between Britain and the United States to the point where the Atlantic would be only a millpond between co-equal and co-prosperous partners. This assumed conditions of free trade and was enshrined in the American Intercourse bill drawn up by the Chancellor of the Exchequer, William Pitt. By its terms the

American States were to maintain their former commercial privileges within the empire, including, of course, the West Indies. The bill was designed to destroy the Navigation Acts; but the old system was stubbornly defended, not least by Lord Sheffield:

the system of courting them [the Americans], lest their trade should take another course, and of treating the Navigation Act as obsolete, impolitic or useless, cannot be attributed to anything but ignorance, levity, or treachery.

Englishmen feared that the Americans would seize the carrying trade: 'not only to the great decrease in our revenue, but the absolute destruction of our navy'. Burke attacked the bill for this reason. The West Indian lobby, anxious for the lower prices which would follow, hoped for the successful passage of the bill, but this was not to be. A truly privileged position was denied the Americans. Both Canada and the West Indies was closed to them; as carriers to Britain they were on an equal footing with European traders, except that their raw materials, especially tobacco, were given special consideration, as were exports from Britain. On these conditions Anglo-American trade became healthy in time. Theoretically the immediate advantage lay with British shipping which alone had access to the West Indies and could fulfill the triangular pattern of trade. In practice the Americans smuggled vast quantities of stores to the islands. Local authorities winked at the practice, and Horatio Nelson, as a local naval enforcement officer, was powerless to prevent the blatant evasion of the law. Supplies cost more as a result of the government's decisions, a factor which hastened the decline of the islands.

New markets were opened by the winning of independence. For the first time Americans had freedom to exploit the markets of the world. Trade flowed to Europe, her empires and the East. With France Americans established a favourable balance of trade, because English manufactures were still preferred to those of France, and longer credit was available in London. The Dutch showed great faith in American capacity for trade and invested in her financial security. The Chinese bought sea otter skins in return for tea. Generally speaking the extent of trade was healthy despite the difficulty in establishing new contacts. The volume of traffic increased at the ports: Boston cleared 42,500 tons in 1772, 55,000 tons in 1788; New York averaged 26,000 tons approximately in 1770–2, remained an occupied city until late 1783, and by 1789 was reckoned to clear over 85,000 tons.

Despite this heartening progress, financial weaknesses, one of the worst legacies of the war, remained. Lack of currency stability had threatened to destroy the patriot cause, and lack of cooperation between States and the use of paper money rather than specie continued to plague the new nation. Inflation and lack of confidence prevailed. Taxation was insufficiently organized and the States fought shy of using the financial expedients so akin to the British method of rule. French money had been invaluable in war, and in peace the Dutch bankers fulfilled a similar role. After Yorktown Robert Morris managed to organize national finance more soundly, but this had no true and assured basis since the confederation government had no independent income. Crises, therefore, regularly occurred.

Financial distress was particularly acute among the people of New England. By 1785 there was overstocking of English goods in the towns and the carrier trade was slack. Farmers also suffered after 1785. Prices fell and heavy taxation and a burden of debt led to a demand for farm relief. These were not farmers like those in the South who could rely on a market for staple crops, but subsistence farmers who sold their limited surplus locally. In Massachusetts during the war their standard of living had dropped and they were unable to meet tax demands in specie. They were not considerately treated by the merchant-dominated assembly and courts. No moratorium on debts was allowed, so in 1786 the farmers resorted to their own form of rough justice. Daniel Shays's rebellion lacked organization and weapons to be effective. The rebels attempted to prevent the courts of justice sitting, and even threatened Boston itself; but authority was not to be so easily defeated. Local militia hunted down the rebels who could not resist the superior armaments used against them. An amnesty was given to the leaders, but many of the farmers had died in the snow on the hills.

Shays's Rebellion gave an impetus to the rethinking of government. Men were worried that civil war would destroy the victory won in 1783, and the emphasis was on a stronger, rather than a looser, form of association. Confederation cannot be deemed a failure, but men were hopeful of greater success under an amended régime.

[30] THE MAKING OF GOVERNMENT

At the outset of the revolution all the States had severed the ties which bound them to London. Connecticut and Rhode Island kept their colonial charters with only modifications until the nineteenth century; Massachusetts drew up a new constitution as late as 1780, but the others had completed the task by the end of 1777. The majority were hardly the enshrinement of democratic principles which might have been expected. Special constitutional conventions were not called and the work was most often undertaken by unrepresentative bodies. Circumstances of war complicated the machinery. Lengthy debates could not be held, nor was it always possible to gain ratification of the constitution by popular consent. One reason for the delay in Massachusetts was the insistence by the people that they would be consulted in the process of drawing up the constitution. Notwithstanding these drawbacks the work was generally well done and has stood the test of time.

In the majority of State constitutions the radicals won a greater measure of power than the conservative patriots, those who wanted to break from Britain and create an American aristocracy or oligarchy. But even the radicals were cautious, and the mood was to acknowledge democratic forces yet seek means to control them. Thus some form of franchise qualification was demanded in every state, and the principle of universal male suffrage was denied. Land was plentiful and comparatively cheap, so some property restrictions were not as disabling as appeared at first sight. At the same time, office holding was still the reserve of

the wealthy in the majority of states, although in cases when the
wealthy were also radical, as with Jefferson and Franklin, this was
not significant. Recognition was given to areas which had hitherto
been under-represented, and this applied particularly to the
frontier which now shared government with the merchants and
established landowners.

The principles of government which Americans sought after
belonged to John Locke and the Baron de Montesquieu. Locke
held the theory of contract between governors and the governed,
the merit of representative institutions and the sanctity of
property; Montesquieu held that the most satisfactory government was achieved when the powers of government – the executive, the legislature and the judiciary – operated separately and
checked each other into perfect balance. English government was
far more interdependent, and the Americans distrusted the
opportunities this gave to tyranny. There was a tendency, however, to lay most emphasis on the legislature, with its democratic
forms. The hierarchical structure of colonial government was
swept away and authority derived ultimately from the voters.
But the continuity with the past is as striking as the differences;
the governors, senates and assemblies were familiar, except that
they now existed by popular right and not by royal grace.

Personal liberties were enshrined in State constitutions. The
State was the government which protected the individual. The
Second Continental Congress had no such profound foundations.
It was a convenient assembly, an expedient which lacked the
dignity of State governments. This is not to underestimate its
achievements; the Declaration of Independence was only the
most obvious. It was the only body which attempted coordination between the States in the war, but a more closely defined
structure was regarded as essential. The Articles of Confederation
were designed to create a body which could resolve issues which
affected the States in common. Drawn up in 1776, it was anticipated that the Articles would be swiftly ratified, and Confederation inaugurated in 1777. The path was less than smooth and,
because all States had to accept the Articles, they did not become
operative until 1781. Stormy debates took place on two crucial

issues: the method of voting, and the distribution of the western lands between the Appalachians and the Mississippi.

Proposals for voting envisaged a single-chamber Congress, each State possessing one vote. The more populous or wealthy states objected violently. Initially they asked for superior voting power to reflect either wealth or population, but later conceded the original proposal. The problem of the western lands was not resolved until 1780 when Congress reversed the Article which had been generally accepted earlier. This had acknowledged that the States with charters giving them the land up to, and in some cases beyond, the Mississippi river, should retain their privileges. States without such charters, Maryland in particular, believed that Congress should administer the newly acquired territory for the common good since it had been won from Britain by the efforts of the whole people. Maryland effectively delayed ratification by her stand on this issue. Support for her action grew, and in 1780 Congress asked the privileged States to surrender their claims to the western lands. Led by New York they all agreed, at least in part, though not all with good grace or unconditionally. Georgia, for example, delayed her surrender until 1802. With the matter at least theoretically solved, Articles of Confederation were ratified in March 1781, giving legal sanction to powers Congress had effectively taken upon itself in 1777.

Under Confederation Congress held limited powers. It could declare war, make treaties, and raise an army and navy, asking for money to pay for them; it could borrow money and regulate coinage; it could establish a post office and supervise Indian affairs; above all it was a forum in which the States could air their grievances. However, there was no executive, no judiciary, and no authority to tax or regulate commerce on a national basis. As Professor Esmond Wright notes: 'in the midst of a war to check tyranny, Americans were suspicious of government even when it was their own'. This failure to give teeth to the national government was deliberate. It reflected a philosophy of decentralization, a philosophy rejected by the makers of the Constitution of 1787. Confederation did not prove an ideal solution to the problems arising from the Declaration of Independence but it was an immediately workable arrangement, and its virtues have been undersung, especially by those who were rooting for the other side. In many ways Confederation was more democratic than the Constitution which followed, sponsored as it was by men like John Jay who believed that 'the people who own the country ought to govern it', and Alexander Hamilton who did not believe that *vox populi* was *vox dei*. He believed that firm government was needed to restrain the passions of men which did not conform to the dictates of reason and justice. The Federalists outgunned their opponents.

One triumph under Confederation was the organization of the western lands. With the cessation of States' claims, Congress was required in the post-war years to police and apportion the land and lay the basis for growth into statehood. Jefferson was responsible for much of the Land Ordinance of 1785 which made provision for the survey and division of the territory into townships six miles square. Each township was divided into thirty-six sections of 640 acres each. Land offices were established to sell lands at not less than one dollar an acre, but in lots of not less than one section. The immediate beneficiaries were, therefore, companies and large landowners who could find the capital.

Only two years later there was the prospect of a quick settlement of the land north of the Ohio river. Congress thus passed the North-West Ordinance (1787) to govern its future. The North-West Territory was to be ruled by a Congressional governor and judges in the first instance; when the population included 5,000 adult males they could elect their own legislature, and send a non-voting delegate to Congress; when there was a population of 60,000 then it would become a State on a par with the original thirteen States. Three, four or five States were envisaged in this vast area. Thus Congress disclaimed all imperial ambitions. Slavery in the lands was expressly forbidden and all human rights considered dear were included: religious freedom, trial by jury and education. In addition:

The utmost good faith shall always be observed towards the Indians; their lands and property shall never be taken from them without their consent; and in their property, rights, and liberty, they shall never be invaded or disturbed.

Congress proved kinder in intent than the American frontiersman in practice.

Congress established a convention in 1787 to amend the Articles of Confederation. Understanding between the States over boundaries and economic matters was not improving, and lack of recognition from European powers, and a belief that Congress was an increasingly unimpressive assembly, led to this decision. To Philadelphia there came delegates with the underlying purpose of writing a new constitution. Not for them a patchwork system to shore up the old edifice. They were men of ability who could well count themselves preeminent: Washington, President of the Convention; James Madison, constitutional lawyer; Alexander Hamilton, lawyer and economist; Benjamin Franklin; John Dickinson — fifty-five members from all States except Rhode Island. Their work was secretly done. Compromise followed compromise to a notable end.

The Federal Constitution of the United States, with the Bill of Rights of 1791, is one of the most workmanlike political testaments in history. Given the age in which it was conceived and the nature of society, it has weathered war and change to a remarkable degree and still operates. It has been severally interpreted, even to the extent of Civil War in 1861, but has proved a malleable instrument in the service of a diverse nation. Comparatively little has been amended and the political stability of America is founded on the constant presence of the Constitution. With its provision of a Senate, where each State was equally represented, and a House of Representatives, where size of population determined representation; with a president, an executive, and a judiciary holding either explicit or implied power which made an effective central government, it cured the major ills of Confederation. With its recognition of the powers of individual States, it maintained the local basis of government.

The evolution of this form of government, accepted by the States and marked by the inauguration of Washington as first President in 1789, completed the work begun by the revolution. The rule of the King of England had been broken; political independence had been established at State level, to be followed by a loose Confederation and finalized in a Federation with the acknowledgement of State rights. Under Washington the Federal government gained strength. Jefferson, his Secretary of State (for Foreign Affairs), believed firmly in the minimal central control, indeed in the minimal government possible. Hamilton, his Secretary of the Treasury, on the other hand pressed for efficiency in government through the widest interpretation of the powers allotted to Congress. For him the Constitution was: 'a fabric which can hardly be stationary, and which will retrograde if it cannot be made to advance'. The two men represented differing ideologies and around them consolidated two political parties; the Republicans, suspicious of central authority, and the Federalists, eager to exploit the powers they had acquired. Later, the Federalist case was assisted by decisions of the Supreme Court under Chief Justice Marshall. Whigs and tories had thus disappeared from America, but the new parties engendered the debate and stimulation required by a healthy body politic.

[31] FOREIGN RELATIONS

The 1783 treaty at Versailles failed to inaugurate an era of goodwill between Britain and the United States. Pitt's attempt to resume trade on generous terms collapsed and the eventual arrangements favoured British merchants. That this trade was essential to the American economy is demonstrated by the fact that in 1790 almost all the foreign shipping entering American ports was British, and nearly fifty per cent of American exports went to the British dominions. Items in the peace treaty were liable to lead to friction, and the weakness of Confederation meant that no diplomatic pressure could be brought to bear upon the contemptuous British government.

First, the northern frontier posts around the Great Lakes, were supposed to be evacuated 'with all convenient speed'. Seven of these forts remained in technically American territory. They supervised the relationship between Indians and fur traders, a group whose interests were abandoned by Shelburne in 1783. Army officers feared that the Indians would become restive if supplies of ammunition and food were suddenly withdrawn. Both military and trading interests, therefore, asked for a gradual retirement, both really loath to relinquish entrenched positions. Until 1796 the forts remained, effectively cutting off American enterprise around the Great Lakes.

Secondly, difficulty was experienced in recovering debts agreed to be repayable by Americans. Weaknesses of the Confederation led to individual States avoiding their responsibilities, which gave the British an excuse to retain the northern posts. Thirdly, boundary disputes flared up at both the eastern and western ends of the treaty line between the United States and Canada. Matters drifted on, with many Englishmen convinced of the immediate demise of the American state.

Partial solutions to these problems were found during Washington's presidency. Alexander Hamilton, who with his economy achieved a sound financial credit, favoured a settlement with the British government. By 1793 the international situation was dominated by the French Revolution and the wars of the First Coalition. Goods in American ships bound for France were seized and the prospect of an Anglo-American war arose. John Jay's treaty of 1794 averted this disaster, although the settlement was too grudging to be considered an adequate basis for a long-term agreement. Debts outstanding from the war for America were to be honoured, the forts south of the Lakes were to be evacuated by 1796; a boundary commission was established; compensation was to be given for the seizure of American ships; and reciprocal commercial arrangements were made. At the same time, however, the Americans recognized the British rights of search and confiscation on the high seas in time of war, and therefore by implication, the right of blockade. Consequently the treaty had a stormy passage through the Senate. Jefferson and the Francophiles found it thoroughly distasteful as it seemed to abandon the French in a manner unworthy of an ally in such recent times. Yet war would have undermined the economy, and war against Britain with her powerful navy was plainly impossible.

Americans continued to covet Canada. This, as much as issues arising from abuse of seapower in the Napoleonic wars, led to the Anglo-American War of 1812. The maritime States, who were most closely affected by the British orders in council and the Napoleonic Berlin and Milan decrees, voted in Congress against war. Although neutral trading with Europe had become exceedingly tricky, they were not prepared to allow the problems of impressment or search to deprive them of trade with Britain. The impetus for war came from States on the frontier. In the north the 'War Hawks' felt threatened by British intrigue with the Indians. Tecumseh's rising in 1811 was the latest, and most spectacular, of raids. In the south the frontiersmen looked for the defeat of Spain, an ally of Britain in the European war. They hoped in particular for the capture of Florida. This so-called 'second war of Independence' disappointed those who had expected most.

Peace came in 1815. Neither Florida nor Canada were won by diplomacy, nor could have been expected. Two minor advantages emerged from the three-year struggle: Indian troubles south of the Great Lakes melted away; the victory of Andrew Jackson at New Orleans in 1815, after the peace had been signed but not communicated, redeemed the dismal military record of the war. Of greater importance, the war was the first national war since the revolution, and it helped to confirm the movement towards unity, despite unrest in New England where secession was openly advocated. It was the last occasion on which the United States fought Britain, and the result in part eradicated the British humiliation at Yorktown. Certainly her triumph in Europe allowed Britain to demand, and obtain, from the Americans the *status quo ante bellum*. Relations between the two nations, however, improved after the war to the extent that the Canadian frontier became demilitarized and disputes were settled by treaty and arbitration rather than force.

France had continued to assist the United States after 1783, but indirectly. As a result of European preoccupation with the French Revolution of 1789, the United States was free to survive the uncertainties of her new Constitution, and to consolidate her power. Sympathy for the revolution in France was muted, indicating the extent of the American retreat into conservatism. Activities of the French minister, Citizen Genêt, in 1793-4 confirmed the American desire for neutrality despite the terms of the alliance of 1778 which was still in force. Genêt sought to enlist Americans into the revolutionary army and navy, and to organize assaults on Spanish and British territory. He even appealed directly to the people without the consent of the government. It was hardly surprising, therefore, that most Americans maintained their support for Washington's Neutrality Proclamation which kept them away from involvement in Europe. The Frenchman's excesses created the atmosphere in which Jay's Treaty, despite its apparent submission to Britain, was in the end acceptable. Jay's Treaty deeply offended French opinion and the preferential treatment which the Americans had enjoyed on the high seas was henceforward denied. A rapid deterioration in Franco-American relations took place and open war seemed imminent. Between 1796 and 1801 the navies of both countries seized the vessels of the other; this was the twilight of war although it did not proceed to open combat. Napoleon was anxious to reverse the hostile policy towards the United States, and in 1801 a new treaty superseded the revolutionary alliance of 1778.

Of greatest significance in postwar affairs between the two countries was the Louisiana Purchase of 1803. The landmass to the west of the Mississippi belonged to Spain when, in 1793, the French revived their vision of a North American empire. At first the French looked to conquest to gain their objective, but after 1796 when the nations allied, negotiations were substituted. In 1803 arrangements were completed and Louisiana became French in return for political power and advantage in Europe for the Spanish royal family. By this transfer the right of American merchants to deposit their wares at New Orleans was placed in jeopardy. It also seemed to threaten the boundaries of the United States, since the ambition of Napoleon was known to be insatiable. The President, Thomas Jefferson, could afford neither war nor inaction. From the suggestion that the French might sell New Orleans, Jefferson was then faced with the offer of the whole of

Louisiana. Napoleon's plan for an American empire based on the West Indies and Louisiana had dramatically folded. He realized that the European peace of 1802 was at best temporary, and concentration on European affairs needed both men and cash. Diversification could not be afforded.

For the sum of $20 million the United States doubled its landmass and assured its control of the North American continent. It was one of the most favourable bargains ever struck. The wealth of America was within her grasp. The Mississippi would never again be disputed territory and the feebleness of Spain could only be to the advantage of the United States. If 1783 guaranteed independence, Louisiana in 1803 laid the foundation for future greatness.

Relations with France remained cordial. Because Britain had the navy to enforce her views on the high seas, the American quarrel lay with her. Napoleon exploited the conflicts which arose over neutral rights and impressment, and Jefferson's policy proved ineffectual. Because of the blockade of Europe, Jefferson, through his Embargo Act of 1807, forbad all exports from the United States hoping to deny Europeans the benefits of the American trade. He only created suffering for his own people; the shipping interests of New England were particularly hard hit. The war of 1812 was caused in part by the French withdrawal of the Berlin and Milan decrees, and the apparent refusal of the British to revoke the orders in council. Yet the war did not assist Napoleon substantially. No longer was Britain his sole opponent. The retreat from Moscow gave new spirit to the major powers and in that crisis America counted for little.

Since 1789 the United States had profited from the upheavals in Europe. She was possibly saved from disaster in the war of 1812 by Britain's preoccupation with European affairs. She certainly gained benefit from the further weakening of Spain in the war. In 1795 Pinckney's Treaty fixed the boundary of West Florida at the latitude of 31° north and obtained for the merchants the right to land ocean-going trade at New Orleans, or some other suitable depot. Spanish control was shattered by the Louisiana purchase of 1803, and she was forced to leave the New

World by the series of rebellions between 1810 and 1826 which won independence for her former colonies. The ideals of the French revolution and her own ineptitude encouraged the uprisings which were able to flourish without undue European interference. Beginning in Caracas, under the leadership of Simon Bolivar, the rebellion, which took on the nature of civil war, was an alternating affair. Not until 1818 was rebel success assured in Venezuela, and elsewhere progress was piecemeal. In 1820 Mexico declared her independence, and the Spanish administration collapsed without a murmur, so it was hardly surprising that in the atmosphere of disintegration, the United States found little difficulty in purchasing Florida from Spain in 1819 for $5 million of outstanding debts.

It was the problem of the break-up of the Spanish empire which provoked a classical statement on American foreign policy in 1823. The Monroe Doctrine advocated a retreat from Europe which marks the end of an epoch in history where Europe and America were intimately connected. In particular it is the end of the era of great wars in America – the Seven Years' War, the American Revolution, and the Napoleonic War of 1812. Earlier, George Washington had made very precise statements on foreign policy in his farewell address in 1796:

The great rule of conduct for us, in regard to foreign nations is, in extending our commercial relations, to have with them as little political connection as possible. . . . Europe has a set of primary interests, which to us have none, or a very remote relation. Hence she must be engaged in frequent controversies, the causes of which are essentially foreign to our concerns. . . . It is our true policy to steer clear of permanent alliances with any portion of the foreign world.

With Spain in the process of being expelled from the New World, isolation seemed a reasonable policy at last. In 1822 the United States recognized the independence of the Argentine, Chile, Peru, Colombia and Mexico, an act of boldness which Britain was unwilling to follow. This was at a time when the forces of reaction in Europe were ascendant; French troops marched into Spain to restore despotic rule and it seemed possible that a combined Franco-Spanish force might seek to reverse the political decisions of the past thirteen years in South America. Monroe, putting aside the suggestion that a joint Anglo-American statement should be made, acted independently and in his Presidential message to Congress in December 1823 warned the European powers that:

The American continents, by the free and independent condition which they have assumed and maintain, are henceforth not to be considered as subjects for future colonization . . . we . . . declare that we should consider any attempt on their part to extend their system to any portion of this hemisphere as dangerous to our peace and safety . . . [and] the manifestation of an unfriendly disposition toward the United States.

The new nation was thus dogmatic and Europe listened; Russia did not prove too troublesome in Alaska, the Canadian border was agreed by discussion and the republics of the south remained free, thanks primarily to British gunboat superiority. By 1823 it was possible to look back on fifty years of successful foreign policy. Wars had been fought and advantage seized through the weaknesses of opponents if not more positively. The United States had established the right to determine her own future.

[32] BRITISH COLONIAL AND FOREIGN POLICY AFTER 1783

With the loss of the American colonies, the first British empire died. Consolation was sought in the knowledge that no longer would America have to be governed or protected, a considerable financial saving. Only the 'barren honour of sovereignty' had been forfeited, but a determination to maintain the rest of the empire inviolate was invariably expressed. No amount of intellectual argument could shake the conviction in the desirability of an imperial policy. Doubt did arise over the future of the empire – would the decline in fortunes apparent since 1775 continue?

Fears for the future were responsible for the niggardly treatment of the United States after 1783 over trading rights. To expose British merchants to competition unnecessarily by the repeal of the Navigation Acts was regarded as madness; after all, the exclusion of the Americans from the privileges of the empire could be considered a positive British advantage from the war.

Recovery was swift in the decade after 1783. This was made possible by the immense economic resources still available, as well as the talents of the Younger Pitt. The nature of the empire shifted. Whereas in 1763 it had been an Anglo-Saxon and western affair, the loss of the American colonies had deprived it of its most precious white and western elements. As a consequence the balance in the empire shifted eastwards towards India, and even before the acquisition of major African territory, it had become an empire of coloured peoples.

Pitt's India Act of 1784 attempted to resolve the problems which the bill presented by Fox the previous year had left unsolved. Both the political and military affairs of the East India Company were subjected to a board of control appointed by the Crown. The board was to consist of ministers who were not, however, to be involved in the distribution of patronage, a task still reserved to the directors of the company. Corruption was to be severely punished and in general the operation of company affairs to be made more responsible in terms of political power. The Governor-General in India, especially after an amendment to the act in 1788, became the crucial figure in the search for justice and efficiency in administration. Until the mutiny of 1857, this remained the pattern of government in India.

Concern for the welfare of Indians was expressed in the course of the trial of Warren Hastings (1788–95) and Professor Harlow points out that during speeches made at the time it was recognized 'that the humane treatment of subject races was not only required by Christian ethics but was also a necessary condition of profitable business'. This self-interested concept of a 'mission of empire' was felt in the context of the east rather than the west; it was the beginning of the white man's burden. It was reflected in English life by the growth of the anti-slavery movement and

despite the seeds of racial superiority which it engendered – 'I
think there is something in our national character and condition
that fits us for this exalted station', as David Laurie observed in
1813 – there was genuine concern for the welfare of bodies and
souls. This was a new argument to add to the old mercantilist
case for an extended empire.

One interesting side-effect of the loss of the American colonies
was the development of Australia. Before 1776 America had been
used as a penal settlement for transported convicts. A fresh
dumping ground had to be found. Proposals to use the coast of
Africa were howled down. 'The gates of hell were there open
night and day to receive the victims of the law', protested Burke,
and the rate of European mortality in Africa justified such
vehemence. Prospects in the Pacific looked brightest. Some form
of settlement there was necessary in any case, before the French
exploited the area opened up by Captian Cook. So, in 1788, the
first detachment of 750 'settlers' guarded by marines and under
the command of Captain Phillip began a new life at Sydney,
New South Wales. The colony prospered on the rich farm land in
the neighbourhood. On the expiration of their sentences the convicts became free settlers, although for many years continuing to
live under military rule.

In the Americas, political trouble in the West Indies was
minimized by absentee landlords and the possibility of slave
risings. Troublemakers were not whites, and so small and isolated were the island units, that any move for independence was
contemptible. Following the French Revolution there were risings
in San Domingo and Haiti, and British owners strongly opposed
all abolitionist measures. The economic wealth of the islands was
still considerable; in 1783 the value of British trade with the
West Indies was £4¼ million which compared with only just over
£2 million with India and £880,000 with her possessions in North
America.

British attention after 1783 was firmly fixed on Canada. Some
Englishmen thought it a shame that Canada had not been lost
along with the other colonies. They saw her indefensible boundaries and gloomily prophesied untold future expense. This,

however, was a minority view. Problems did exist, and the War of 1812 was caused partly by the weakness of her frontier with the United States. More immediately, the influx of United Empire Loyalists from the south threatened to disrupt the system created by the Quebec Act of 1774, with its recognition of French forms for the Roman Catholic settlers. This did not apply to the settlers in Nova Scotia, New Brunswick or the islands off the coast – they were given a measure of self-government in territory not covered by the Act. But the 10,000 Loyalists who settled in Ontario found both the political and social arrangements alien to their experience. Pitt delayed his solution until 1791 when the Canada Act divided Quebec into Upper and Lower Canada, based on an approximate racial division between Anglo-Saxon Protestants and French Roman Catholics. The need for parliamentary institutions was recognized, but care was taken to prevent the elected assemblies seizing power from the Governor and his executive, as had happened in the pre-revolutionary era. In each province two assemblies were created: one was elected, the other nominated, approximating to the House of Commons and the House of Lords. Indeed, the Governor was given powers to create an aristocracy, a forlorn attempt to counteract some of the revolutionary blasts from across the English Channel, let alone from the United States. In addition there was a nominated Executive Council of members who could, if the Governor so wished, be drawn from the assemblies. By strengthening the non-popular elements in government, and maintaining control from London, Pitt hoped to create a perfect balance in the constitution. Despite the inevitable frictions which arose, the system worked creditably well for fifty years, until it was modified by the changing climate of British politics after 1832. Lord Durham's report in 1839 led to the reunification of Lower and Upper Canada and eventually Canada evolved to Dominion status, entirely responsible for her own affairs.

It is not possible to leave consideration of the relationship between Britain and her colonies in the post-war era without reference to that most troublesome of her possessions, Ireland. The development of Ireland towards independence although encouraged by the extent of self-government in 1782, was rudely shattered by the Act of Union in 1801. The independent Irish Parliament was destroyed by its own exclusiveness and by the fear that republican sympathy would eventually remove Ireland from the empire altogether. Failure was already apparent by 1785 when Pitt offered the Irish a favourable commercial agreement if their external affairs were settled in London. Opposition in Ireland and the House of Commons forced him to shelve the matter, and a chance was lost. After 1789 revolutionary ideas further bedevilled the relationship. Grattan's Parliament was never in any sense democratic, and Catholics in particular, seventy-five per cent of the population, were denied political rights. Internal unrest was widespread, caused by the despotic nature of the governing class, and in 1791 Wolfe Tone organized a Society of United Irishmen composed of Anglicans, Presbyterians and Catholics to press for reform. In 1793 Catholics were allowed to vote, but this failed to alleviate discontent which culminated in the rising of 1798. Without French assistance it was doomed from the start, and was put down with cruelty. It led to the Act of Union which was an admission of failure, and a legacy in which statesmen floundered for over a century. Pitt hoped to advance Catholics into political partnership, but others were more concerned to destroy Irish pretensions.

In Europe Britain looked for new allies. Hopelessly isolated during the American war, she was now helped by events in the Netherlands, 1785-7. The Prince of Orange was restored as Stadholder and in 1788 Pitt made an alliance with the United Provinces and Prussia. This triple alliance was strong enough to intervene successfully in the Baltic to enforce Danish neutrality in the war between Sweden and Russia. Peace between the two belligerents followed the Swedish defeat in 1790. In the same year the alliance attempted to settle the affairs of the recently deceased Joseph II of Austria, and to effect peace between Russia and Turkey. Failure led to the slackening of ties between Prussia and Britain, but as late as 1792 Pitt was unruffled by the international situation.

Although Pitt was prepared to go to war with France over the

Netherlands, he signed a commercial treaty in 1786 which sweetened the air. Principles of free trade were admitted, a policy giving greater advantages to Britain than to France. Generally in the period after 1783 France could not afford an aggressive foreign policy; and the revolution of 1789 seemed to simplify the role of Britain in Europe by removing into civil war her most dangerous foe. Both the economic and financial policy of Pitt needed conditions of peace in which to flourish, and it was with reluctance that he entered the revolutionary wars in 1793.

Between 1789 and 1793 serious diplomatic troubles arose with Spain over rights of settlement on Vancouver Island, at Nootka Sound. British merchant vessels had been seized by the Spaniards, whose territory effectively ceased far to the south on the west coast of America. Spain claimed sovereignty as far north as latitude 60° and wished to exclude the British from the area entirely. Although relations between the two countries had been cordial hitherto, Pitt could not ignore this provocation. With support from her new European allies, Britain stood firm in 1790; Spain failed to rally support from France, Austria or Russia and knew that the United States would seize New Orleans given a suitable pretext. She had little option in backing down to allow British subjects to settle in coastal places not already occupied.

Thus, by 1793, with allies, the advantage of trade with the United States and with her empire flourishing anew, Britain could claim greatness again. She had sloughed off her humiliation at the loss of America with skill and yet without undue difficulty. Her capacity for expansion was to be realized over the next sixty years, her industry and her empire complementing each other.

[33] DEMOCRACY AND AMERICA

The effect of the American Revolution upon European thought was immediate, although it was by no means the only factor which worked towards violent change. Professor Palmer points out that the revolution coincided with the climax of the Age of Enlightenment; it showed that many of the ideals of the philosophers could be put into practice. Religious freedom, responsible citizenship and written constitutions were all attempted in the United States and justified half a century of theorizing. This created new hope in Europe among those who sought to implement change. American forms showed up the inadequacies of hereditary government and the denial of justice. Already by 1786 the France of Louis XVI was in the process of adaptation, but the lessons of the New World were most deeply appreciated in circles outside the court.

Of all European countries, France learned most. Lafayette, who had enlisted for America to fight England rather than as a proof of abstract ideals, learned to love and respect liberty during the course of the war. French soldiers generally were influenced by the republican forms around them, and brought home a favourable view of America which may have influenced men's decisions to support the revolution in their own districts in 1789. Americans in Paris also influenced French opinion. Between 1776 and 1785, the indefatigable Franklin was the most highly respected foreigner in the country. He deliberately popularized America in conversations and writing. Jefferson carried on this task after the peace at Versailles. He tried to consolidate the truth and eliminate erroneous views and encourage French authors to write on American topics. In 1789 he was sought out for advice in the early days of the revolution.

Jacques-Pierre Brissot showed the extent of American influence. He founded an abortive Gallo-American society, and visited the United States, once during the debates on the Federal constitution, returning to France to apply the forms he had witnessed. He was anxious that the people should continue to exercise more direct control on government than was apparent in

America, and thus indirectly he encouraged perpetual turbulence in political affairs rather than their stabilization. Only when he became virtual head of the state in 1792 did he realize the impossibility of his earlier beliefs. In fact the French Revolution ran a very different course from its American predecessor; it was an altogether more profound affair. Far more fundamental tasks had to be attempted in 1789. Social, economic and political feudalism needed to be overthrown, whereas the Americans had modified and developed English forms which had emerged in the Glorious Revolution of 1688-9. Condorcet pointed to specific abuses which existed in France – the clergy and aristocracy in separate privileged orders in the state, insidious tax exemptions and vicious collection, and the failure to obtain justice. These had no direct parallel in America in 1775.

Probably the most obvious American influence in the early days of the 1789 revolution was on the *Declaration of the Rights of Man*, that supreme charter of political beliefs in modern western civilization. It bears a close resemblance to the American documents, especially that of Virginia, which cast off British rule in 1776. The parallel cannot be forced too far, and the American ideas were developed in the European context. Yet it does show that there was an Atlantic community which shared its political beliefs, or at least could not ignore its neighbours.

On the rest of Europe American democracy had less profound effects, although the age 1776-99 was fraught with revolutionary activity and temporary successes were often forthcoming. In Holland, where John Adams laboured long for financial assistance and backed the anti-Orange party, sympathizers organized themselves into militia bands to win a degree of freedom. Ireland witnessed a similar upsurge of democratic fervour backed by military force, again achieving a limited success. England was affected, but the Yorkshire Association, influenced by the democratic breeze wafting across the Atlantic, remained a peaceful pressure group. Discussions in Germany were invariably academic and obscure. Of the 30,000 German troops who had fought in America, 12,000 remained behind as settlers; of those who returned many held conservative views. Certainly the Germans never held the passionate views on America which often gripped the French, who were sometimes more inclined to favour Americans because they so loathed the British. In Italy and Spain little of importance was allowed to circulate in print.

Throughout the whole of Europe the primary means of communication was the press – books, pamphlets and newspapers. The growth of the press was indeed noteworthy, especially the publication of newspapers. For example, 1,225 new periodicals appeared in Germany in the 1780s. Masonic lodges also flourished at this time and encouraged the ideal of an international and classless fellowship. Both Washington and Franklin were masons, and were highly regarded by their European counterparts.

Independence sentiments in South America stemmed from the French Revolution rather than the American. The degree of separation between the United States and nations to the south was indeed remarkable. Contact was minimal. American distrust was engendered by the abolition of slavery by the French Convention in 1794 and subsequent disorders in the Caribbean. White refugees arrived in the southern States to escape the reign of terror, and brought with them fears of slave insurrection. Coupled with the new economic desirability of slavery, these fears led to a hardening of race relations in the South.

But what of democracy within the United States after 1789? Did it remain a formidable ideal for the young nation? A summary of progress is available in the writings of Alexis de Tocqueville (1805–59), Frenchman, count, lawyer, politician and historian. He published his *Democracy in America* in two parts, in 1835 and 1840, after a year's travel through the country. The work was, and still is, regarded as a masterpiece. More interested in democracy than America, he shrewdly investigated its operation showing both its anatomy and applying lessons to the European scene.

He noted that political democracy in practice was far from perfect. For example, the electorate often failed to choose the most able men to represent them. Sometimes this stemmed from a distrust of cleverness, but also from the unwillingness of able men to stand for office because personal rewards were insufficient.

Elected representatives were likely to become demogogues, and long-term appointments would produce frustration in those excluded from office; yet frequent elections would lead to instability. Tocqueville also denied that popular government was the most economical. In order to satisfy the demands of the electorate, public funds had to be spent on social improvements which would drain the national resources. He also predicted that the foreign policy of a democracy would be confused, liable to excess of national pride or shortsightedness, although here he could not point to America since she had retreated into isolation.

Distinctions are made between American and European political forms. In particular Tocqueville saw that political parties in America lacked that ideological conflict which still made revolution in Europe likely. American democracy, with a broadly based suffrage, led to opinions being freely expressed within a number of parties. No party existed to challenge the legality of government, and in the early days of the Constitution all parties agreed to make the system work. In France, however, political parties were prepared to use physical force to implement policies if they were defeated in debate. Although the body politic might be weakened by a number of conflicting views, it was healthier that major clashes be avoided. This was possible in the American context with a tradition of sophisticated parliamentary discussions on the British pattern.

Political democracy seemed preferable to the alternatives, monarchy and aristocracy. Tocqueville believed that men should exercise political rights in order to understand the idea of liberty, to mature as political creatures and to develop a sense of morality in terms of the rule of law, reason and humanity. In this way the need for free associations and the advantages of cooperation would be realized. By being involved in making decisions men would be educated in the process, developing their sense of justice and discrimination. The press in America and France reflected these ideals. In Paris the press was politically disruptive – elsewhere the press was weak; by contrast, although the American press was often violent in tone, yet it enjoyed the assurance of freedom. It was more locally based and reflected differing views which, if not chanelled into the press, could lead to violent physical demonstrations.

The sovereignty of the people and the freedom of the press are therefore entirely correlative; censorship and universal suffrage are on the other hand contradictory.

Democracy was social as well as political. There were still social groupings in America, but they were, and still are, more flexible than in Europe. A hereditary aristocracy allowed limited flexibility (usually through marriage or royal appointment) whereas in America the division of wealth or intellectual attainment cut across birth and allowed of no special privileges. All men were gentlemen with opinions to be aired, criticized and respected.

They establish temporary distinctions, and do not establish classes properly so called . . . at bottom they feel themselves equal, and are. In vain does wealth and poverty, authority and subordination accidentally place a great distance between two men, for public opinion, which is founded on the ordinary order of things, draws them to a common level, and creates between them a sort of imaginary equality, in spite of the real inequality of conditions.

The effect of democracy in social terms was the development of neighbourliness. Americans were found by Tocqueville to be more responsive than Englishmen on casual acquaintance. Their manners were easier and less bound by social etiquette. At the same time they could be more selfish for personal advancement and in the pursuit of material well-being. Pure science and the arts in America were not so successful, and Tocqueville feared that the repression of individualism and the substitution of a general mediocrity would be the greatest of all evils which could emanate from a democracy.

Despite its shortcomings, the Frenchman believed democracy to be worth close study by all Europeans:

To those for whom the word 'democracy' is synonomous with disturbance, anarchy, spoliation and murder, I have attempted to show that the government of democracy may be reconciled with respect for property, with defence for rights, with safety to freedom, with reverence to religion; that if democratic government is less favourable than another to some of the finer parts of human nature, it has also great and noble elements; and that, perhaps, after all, it is the will of God to shed a lesser grade of happiness on the totality of mankind, not to combine a greater share of it on a smaller number, or to raise the few to the verge of perfection.

Although the peacefulness of American democracy was shattered by the Civil War, the advantages of the system have been proved. Written constitutions have been made to work; under them a people has prospered. No greater justification can be produced for the decision of the colonists to fight in 1775.

Further Reading (1775–87)

Books marked with an asterisk contain more extensive bibliographies which are immensely helpful. Some of the volumes in the earlier list of further reading (pp. 115 and 116) also deal with events in the period 1775–87.

General surveys

*J. R. ALDEN, The American Revolution 1775–83. Harper Torchbooks (paperback) (New York & London, 1954).

*PIERS MACKESY, The War for America 1775–83. Longmans (London, 1964).

A. GOODWIN (ed.), 'The New Cambridge Modern History' Vol VIII, The American and French Revolutions. Cambridge University Press (Cambridge, 1965).

R. R. PALMER, The Age of Democratic Revolution: 1760–1800, 2 vols. Princeton University Press (Princeton, N.J., 1959, 1964).

Documents

R. BIRLEY, Speeches and Documents in American History, Vol I, 1776–1815. Oxford University Press 'World's Classics' (London, 1944).

HENRY S. COMMAGER, Documents in American History. Appleton-Century-Croft (New York, 7th ed., 1963).

Specific aspects of the period
Political and constitutional
E. C. BURNETT, *The Continental Congress*. Macmillan (London, 1941).

The Period of Confederation
M. JENSEN, *The New Nation 1781–89*. Knopf (New York, 1950).

Foreign affairs
S. F. BEMIS, *The Diplomacy of the American Revolution*. Oliver & Boyd (Edinburgh, 1935).
S. F. BEMIS, *A Diplomatic History of the United States*. Holt (New York, 1946).

Political thought
A. DE TOCQUEVILLE, *Democracy in America* [1835–1840]. Oxford University Press 'World's Classics' abridged ed., (London, 1946).

British History

H. BUTTERFIELD, *George III, Lord North and the People 1779–80*. Bell (London, 1949).
I. R. CHRISTIE, *The End of North's Ministry 1780–82*. Macmillan (London, 1958).
J. HOLLAND ROSE (ed.), *The Cambridge History of the British Empire*, Vol. II, *1783–1870*. Cambridge University Press (Cambridge, 1940).

Biography

W. B. WILLCOX, *Portrait of a General: Sir Henry Clinton*. Knopf (New York, 1965).
A. O. ALDRIDGE, *Thomas Paine, Man of Reason*. Cresset Press (London, 1960).

Pamphlet

W. R. BROCK, *The Effect of the loss of the American Colonies upon British Policy*. Historical Association (1957).

AMERICAN AFFAIRS	BRITAIN, THE EMPIRE AND EUROPE

PEACE OF PARIS

1763	**1763**
	April. Grenville, First Minister
	John Wilkes; case of
May. Pontiac's Rebellion	No. 45 *North Briton*
October. Proclamation Act	
1764	**1764**
March. Sugar Act	
Currency Act	April. Alliance of Frederick II of Prussia with Catherine II of Russia
1765	**1765**
March. Stamp Act	
Quartering Act	July. Marquis of Rockingham First Minister
October. Stamp Act Congress meets	
1766	**1766**
March. Repeal of Stamp Act	
Declaratory Act	July. Chatham, First Minister
1767	
May. Townshend Duties	
1768	**1768**
February. Massachusetts Circular Letter	March. John Wilkes and the Middlesex Election

August. Non-importation
  begins
October. Arrival of British
  troops in Boston

November. Grafton, First
  Minister

1770

1770

March. Partial repeal of
  Townshend duties
  Boston Massacre
August. End of Non-
  Importation Agreements

February. Lord North,
  First Minister

December. Fall of Choiseul,
  French Minister of
  Foreign Affairs

1772
June. *Gaspee* burnt

1772

December. Boston Committee
  of Correspondence
  established

August. Partition of Poland

1773
May. Lord North's Tea Act

1773

June. Regulating Act for
  India
  Warren Hastings, First
  Governor-General

December. Boston Tea Party

1774
March. Coercive Acts

1774

May. Accession of Louis XVI
  of France
  Vergennes, Minister of
  Foreign Affairs
July. Treaty of Kutchuk-
  Kainardji between
  Russia and Turkey

June. Quebec Act

September. First Continental
  Congress

October. Adoption of
   Continental Association

1775
February. North's
   Conciliatory Proposals
April. Lexington and Concord
May. Second Continental
   Congress
June. Bunker Hill
October. Invasion of Canada

1776
January. *Commonsense*
   published
March. British evacuation of
   Boston
July. Declaration of
   Independence
August. Howe on Long Island

December–January 1777.
   American military success
   at Trenton and Princeton

1777
September. Howe takes
   Philadelphia
October. Burgoyne surrenders
   at Saratoga
Washington winters at
   Valley Forge

1778

May. Clinton replaces Howe
   British withdrawal from
   Philadelphia

1776

October. Necker, Director of
   Treasury in France

1778
Volunteer organizations in
   Ireland (1778–9)
February. France allies with
   United States

December. Expedition to
South; Georgia taken

1779

July–August. Estaing and
French fleet off New York
and Savannah

1780

May. British capture
Charleston
July. Rochambeau and
French army in New
England
August. Battle of Camden
September. Arnold's defection
to Britain
October. Battle of King's
Mountain

1781

March. British victory at
Guilford Court House

July. Drawn naval battle
off Ushant
War of Bavarian
Succession

1779
June. Spain declares war
on Britain
July. France captures
Granada
August. Franco-Spanish
attempted invasion of
England
John Paul Jones off coasts
of Britain

1780
January. Relief of Gibraltar
March. Rodney in West
Indies
April. Dunning's Resolutions

June. Gordon Riots
July. Haidar Ali attacks
Madras

August. Armed Neutrality
of the North

December. Britain declares
war on Holland

1781
February. St Eustatius
captured from Dutch
May. Spain takes Florida
Fall of Necker in France
July. Eyre Coote defeats
Haidar Ali at Porto Novo

October. Yorktown

1782

November. Peace
Preliminaries signed at
Versailles

1783

September. Definitive Peace
at Versailles

1782
February. Spain takes
Minorca
March. Second Rockingham
Administration
April. Battle of the Saints
May. Independent Irish
Parliament
July. Shelburne
Administration
September. Siege of
Gibraltar

1783
April. Fox-North Coalition

Index